Sparse Distributed Memory

Sparse Distributed Memory

Pentti Kanerva

A Bradford Book
The MIT Press
Cambridge, Massachusetts
London, England

© 1988 Massachusetts Institute of Technology

All rights reserved. No part of this book may be reproduced in any form by any electronic or mechanical means (including photocopying, recording, or information storage and retrieval) without permission in writing from the publisher.

This book was set in Palatino by Asco Trade Typesetting Ltd. in Hong Kong and printed and bound by Halliday Lithograph in the United States of America.

Library of Congress Cataloging-in-Publication Data

Kanerva, Pentti.
  Sparse distributed memory.

  "A Bradford book."
  Bibliography: p.
  Includes index.
  1. Memory—Computer simulation. 2. Neural computers. 3. Artificial intelligence.
I. Title.
QP406.K36   1988   153.1'2   88-685
ISBN 0-262-11132-2

*To you, Dianne,
for your love,
for your struggle for life,
and for your insight into people.*

Contents

Foreword by Douglas R. Hofstadter   xi
Preface   xix

Introduction   1
Perspective   6
Background   7
Premises   13
Symbols   14

Chapter 1
Mathematical Foundations   15
The Space $\{0, 1\}^n$ 15
Concepts Related to the Space $\{0, 1\}^n$ 15
Some Properties of the Space $\{0, 1\}^n$ 18
Memory Items as Points of the Space $\{0, 1\}^n$ 23
Sets, Sequences or Lists, and Multisets   26

Chapter 2
Background Material from Computers   29
The Random-Access Memory of a Computer   30
Content-Addressable Memories   33

Chapter 3
Background Material from Idealized Neurons   35
The Neuron   35
Formal Neurons   35
Modeling with Neurons: The Perceptron   37
A Critical Look at Perceptron-Convergence Learning   39

Chapter 4
Neurons as Address Decoders   43
Input Coefficients and the Address of a Neuron   43

viii   Contents

The Threshold and the Response Region of a Neuron   44
Unequal Weights and Weighted Distance   46

Chapter 5
Search of Memory for the Best Match   49
The Problem of the Best Match   49
The Best-Match Machine   50
A Note on Serial and Parallel Computing   52

Chapter 6
Sparse Memory   53
Concepts Related to Sparse Memory   54
The Nearest-Neighbor Method in Sparse Memory   56

Chapter 7
Distributed Storage   61
Concepts Related to Distributed Storage   62
The Feasibility of Distributed Storage: Finding the Best Match   65
Further Concepts and Properties of Distributed Storage   71
Interpretations   76

Chapter 8
Storage and Retrieval of Sequences: Predicting   79
General Data Storage   79
Storage of Sequences   80
Convergence to the Stored Sequence   82
Second- and Higher-Order Prediction: k-fold Prediction   83
Interpretations   86

Chapter 9
Constructing Distributed Memory   87
An Important Detail of Architecture   90
Cerebellar Cortex as a Random-Access Memory   90

Chapter 10
The Organization of an Autonomous Learning System   97
Memory for Patterns and Pattern Sequences   97
Modeling the World   99
Storing the World Model in Sparse Distributed Memory   100
Including Action in the World Model   103
Learning to Act   106
Learning in Social Settings   110

Application to the Frame Problem of Robotics 112
The Encoding Problem 116
Summary and Conclusions 118

Appendix A
The Distribution of the Third Side of a Triangle 121

Appendix B
The Intersection of Two Circles 125

Appendix C
The Fidelity of Sparse Distributed Memory 135

Appendix D
The Distance between Two Read Chains 139

Appendix E
Commonly Used Symbols 143

Bibliography 147
Index 151

Foreword

To understand human memory is to understand what concepts are: how they are stored and retrieved, how they overlap with and trigger one another. And it does not take much thought to recognize that understanding the nature of concepts is nothing short of understanding the essence of the mental. Thus, a complete theory of memory would not merely be a theory of one aspect of mind; it would be a complete theory of mind.

This beautiful little book by Pentti Kanerva represents a significant step in that direction. It presents a simple and elegant mathematical theory accounting for many aspects of the remarkable fluidity of human memory.

Rather than summarizing Kanerva's theory, I will take the opportunity to present a few examples of the types of memory phenomena that the theory was inspired by and that it addresses, since Kanerva himself is somewhat terse on that subject. The types of phenomena that I list below, though they are commonplace, never fail to impress me with their extraordinary richness, subtlety, and variety. Only recently have researchers like Kanerva begun to conceive of ways that a physical device could possibly exhibit behavior so flexible. Here, then, is a short list of some of my favorite memory phenomena:

- I begin with the nearly trivial observation that members of a familiar perceptual category automatically evoke the name of the category. Thus, when we see a staircase (say), no matter how big or small it is, no matter how twisted or straight, no matter how ornamented or plain, modern or old, dirty or clean, the label "staircase" spontaneously jumps to center stage without any conscious effort at all. Obviously, the same goes for telephones, mailboxes, milkshakes, butterflies, model airplanes, stretch pants, gossip magazines, women's shoes, musical instruments, beachballs, station wagons, grocery stores, and so on. This phenomenon, whereby an external physical stimulus indirectly activates the proper part of our memory, permeates human life and language so thoroughly that most people have a hard time working up any interest in it, let alone

astonishment, yet it (together with its close cousins, described below) is probably the most key of all mental mechanisms.
- A close cousin to the ability just mentioned is that of putting adjectival or "style" labels on fresh percepts, such as the ability to look at a painting and name the artist, or to hear a piece of music and name the composer or performer or style. We can recognize that an accent is Spanish, that the weather is threatening, that a child is sluggish, that a room is messy, that a skyscraper is Art Deco, that a street is tawdry, and so on. This ability extends into all types of realms, so that one football coach might recognize another coach's style merely from watching a team play for a few minutes! Once again, external stimuli trigger activity in just the right areas of our memories.
- The just-mentioned ability blurs rather smoothly into the ability to assign labels to intangible, nonperceptual phenomena. Thus, most adults in our culture can easily recognize instances of such abstract conceptual phenomena as black humor, white lies, gray areas, red tape, green thumbs, blue funks, corny jokes, stage fright, peer pressure, civil wars, double-crossers, inferiority complexes, slapstick comedy, euphemistic language, procrastination, and on and on. It is worth pointing out that even the retrieval from memory of the name of *any verb*, such as "crawl", "dangle", "besmirch", and so on, is an act of highly abstract categorization.

  Sometimes the labels we assign to intangible items are proper nouns: a new war is called "another Viet Nam", a new fundamentalist tyrant is called "another Khomeini", and so forth. Journalists and P.R. people seem especially fond of using colorful descriptive phrases, such as "the Beirut of professions", "the Muhammad Ali of surrealism", "the Cadillac of vodkas", "the Watergate of France", "the Marie Curie of cognitive science", and so on—but we are all prone to coming up with such phrases, and they crop up naturally in our everyday speech without conscious exertion.
- Our propensity to describe things as "another Edsel", "a veritable Mozart", or "the latest Hula Hoop" is a facet of our insuppressible tendency to be reminded of one thing by another. Meeting someone new, we are reminded of a friend. Walking through a new city, we are reminded of familiar cities. When something new happens to us, we are reminded of other things that happened to us, sometimes long ago and far away. Dinner-party conversations take random walks through events and ideas in a manner determined by the associative networks of the participants. Similarly, joke-tellers can banter back and forth forever, saying, "Yeah, that reminds me of the

one about the drunk monkey who ...,," where the connections often reside at very high levels of abstraction.

This abstract reminding ability shades into the ability to construct interesting analogies. For example, I once congratulated a friend who had just swum 17 laps of a pool, 16 of whose laps made a mile, by saying, "Congratulations—you've just swum a guinea!" (a reference to the British monetary unit of that name, whose value is 21 shillings: one pound plus one shilling). The thought had come unbidden to me; it just sprang into my mind at the moment I began speaking. This analogy is simple, but sometimes the analogies that come via everyday reminding experiences are far from obvious, and can have significant consequences: a man's decision about whether to quit his job may be greatly influenced by his having recently witnessed from up close what happened to a friend who left her mate. The situations are not by any means identical, but the analogy may be strong and impressive enough to add weight to one side or the other.

On a grander scale, nearly all political decisions are based on analogy. Political leaders constantly ask themselves, in effect, "Is this situation we are faced with today like ones we know about from the past, and whose consequences we know?" Which situations come to mind, and how strongly one believes in their relevance to the situation at hand, is determined by how one's memory catalogues and stores situations—which aspects are remembered, which ones forgotten, how much weight each is given, and so on.

- Much of our linguistic ability resides at the supra-word level—at the level of idiomatic phrases of various sorts. What types of situations inspire one to come out with phrases like, "Oh, they're *a dime a dozen*", "He's *a royal pain in the neck*", "She didn't *bat an eyelash*", and so on? Such linguistic units act in many ways just like "big words," and effectively increase any estimate of our vocabulary by a large amount. But just like words for the most concrete of categories—"dog", "chewing gum"—these superwords should be thought of as designating abstract categories whose instances come in many varieties, each of which is capable of unconsciously and rapidly triggering recall of the category name.

- The complexity of this "superword" facility that all mature language-users enjoy is strikingly highlighted when two or more such phrases are simultaneously retrieved and unconsciously spliced together to form a "syntactic blend"—a novel hybrid phrase that most speakers and listeners will not even notice. A typical example is the italicized phrase at the end of the following sentence I once overhead: "Back in those days, the City Lights clerks often saw poor beatniks walking out with poetry books under their arm without paying for them, and they would generally *turn the other eye*". This is a hybrid consisting of influences drawn from several stock phrases known to the speaker, including "turn the other cheek", "turn a blind eye", "look the other way", and perhaps more. Incidentally, neither the speaker nor the listener batted an eyelash when this was said.

It is hard for most people to believe that speakers and listeners are generally quite unaware of uttering or understanding such phrases. However, one can train oneself to "keep an ear peeled" for such phrase-blends, and one quickly discovers how astonishingly prevalent the phenomenon is, yet—even more astonishingly—how most people almost never notice it. In fact, it is amusing that non-native speakers of English, when given a few examples in English and asked to look out for instances of the same phenomenon in their language, predictably reply, "Oh, but we don't make such mistakes in our language!"—as if the memory mechanisms underlying that type of mental operation were unique to the brains of native English speakers!

- There are many types of strangely creative uses of language that verge on error. A typical example, familiar to everyone, is when a teacher unconsciously begins a lecture with "Yesterday, we were talking about memory mechanisms"—meaning not really "yesterday" but the previous class meeting, which might have occurred two days ago, three days ago, or even a week ago. Such liberties are taken all the time with language, sometimes deliberately but more often unconsciously.

  A related phenomenon is the effortless extension of familiar idioms by lightly "tweaking" them, as in the phrase "keep an ear peeled", which I used above, or as in this pair of related examples: "The Chinese chefs in this town have been playing musical restaurants recently" and "It seems like college presidents are playing musical universities these days".

- In general, the careful collection and analysis of errors constitutes one of the most interesting ways to probe memory. Here is a highly provocative yet typical example of a memory malfunction: A friend who was rather tired wanted to look up the Yiddish word for "February". He picked up his English-Yiddish dictionary, and proceeded to look under the letter "B" instead of "F". Why "B"? Because "B" is the second letter of the alphabet—and February is the second month of the year! He was quite tired, but that fact by no means renders the event invalid as an example. In fact, quite the contrary—only through such extreme malfunctions can we begin to sense just how complexly organized and cross-indexed is our conceptual repertoire; and then the question is, "If there are so many routes of access threading through our minds, how come memory is so accurate and so efficient 99 percent of the time?"

- Then there is the notorious "tip of the tongue" phenomenon, where we are certain that we know the exact word or name for something but, maddeningly, we just cannot come up with it, no matter how hard we try. Related to this is the partial-retrieval phenomenon, in which we get a distinct sense that "the name has two syllables," "it sounds something like 'Bonner,'" "I think it begins with an M," and so on.

- Finally, I am fascinated by the often highly creative process of "diffusion" or spreading out in idea space, by which I mean the process whereby a specific idea gradually becomes more and more general. Sometimes this process takes place inside an individual mind; other times it is a collective process that takes place in a pool of communicating minds.

A favorite example is the "Rubik's Cube" concept. When the cubes were first released on the market in 1980, the term "Rubik's Cube" meant exactly one thing and no more. But over a period of just a few months after its release, the collective minds of inventors and marketers generalized it, first along one conceptual dimension, then along another and then another. First there were strangely colored or painted cubes, then came corner-shaved Rubik's cubes, then spherical Rubik's cubes, $2 \times 2 \times 2$ Rubik's cubes, $4 \times 4 \times 4$ Rubik's cubes. Eventually we were flooded with Rubikian tetrahedra, octahedra, dodecahedra, and icosahedra. Meanwhile, mathematical types dreamed up such notions as four-dimensional Rubik's cubes, irregular solids à la Rubik, skew-sliced Rubikian cubes, and on and on. After but a few months, the initial idea was now merely the nucleus of a vast swarm of similar ideas extending outward with no well-defined edge.

Of all the mental phenomena I have described, this one is the least obviously related to memory. The connection becomes clearer, however, when one realizes that it is all about how concepts change over time: a given concept expands, comes to have new overlaps, triggers the retrieval of yet other concepts, and around and around it goes.

This list by no means exhausts the diversity of memory phenomena, but it certainly hints at the richness of the subject. I hope that readers who were skeptical about the first paragraph of this foreword will now be more inclined to take it seriously. On the other hand, neither I nor Pentti Kanerva would claim that his work represents an explanation of all these intriguing and challenging facets of memory. Rather, his work is a theory of associative retrieval and storage that allows one to gain a *glimmer* of an understanding of how these extremely complex and subtle phenomena might take place in a human brain. Specifically, the model affords a detailed and highly plausible explanation of how humans can (and machines might) retrieve the memory most appropriate to a given situation, even when the match between that memory and the given situation is far from exact.

Although I said I would not describe Kanerva's theory, I would at least like to whet readers' appetites. The whole thing revolves around the elegant mathematical properties of the space of all possible bit-strings—sequences of ones and zeros—of a given length (typically 1,000 or more). Such mathematical concepts as "nearness", "neighborhood", "sphere", and so on are the central notions explored. Why would this kind of thing be at all relevant to a theory about human memory? Because, as Kanerva and many other people have argued, it is highly plausible that in the brain, items stored into and retrieved from memory are indeed very large sets of binary on-off features—in short, long bit-strings. It is obvious, therefore, that if one has a deep understanding of the mathematics of such spaces of bit-strings—in particular, the properties of such concepts as "nearness" and "degree of overlap of neighborhoods"—one will have a handle on the meaning of terms such as "conceptual nearness" and "conceptual overlap", which are the very crux of all memory phenomena.

Once the identification of diffuse, overlapping concepts with regions inside a space of bit-strings has been clearly established, the rest of Kanerva's theory is concerned with a detailed description of physical hardware in which such a space, despite its astronomical size, can actually be realized in a practical way, and that allows its wonderful mathematical properties to be taken advantage of. The hardware described is surprisingly close to same of the low-level circuitry of today's computer memories, but a twist in the way the machinery is used gives it utterly novel and fluid properties, totally contrasting with the usual rigid behavior of computer memories.

Developing and communicating such abstruse ideas is not all trivial, and a treatise of this sort could easily be rendered opaque to all but a tiny coterie of specialists. This tends, most unfortunately, to be the way science is done. Luckily, Pentti Kanerva has none of that tendency. His desire is for maximum clarity, and he takes great pains to make the presentation of his research as crystal-clear and elegant as the research itself. When I first read this work in its incipient form, back in 1977, I was greatly impressed by the way in which Kanerva transmitted to me his own geometrical intuition for the high-dimensional spaces with which he is dealing. The phenomena became almost as visualizable as if they were merely three-dimensional. I would say that anyone who understands binary numbers and the rudiments of computer architecture can follow the essence of his theory.

One of the beauties of scientific research is how, on occasion, completely unrelated ideas come together in a perfect harmony. One such coincidence took place in the development of this theory. One day, Kanerva quite by chance came across some schematic pictures of the human cerebellum in *Scientific American*—pictures that looked remarkably similar to his own wiring diagrams of a hypothetical computer architecture to implement his memory model. At that time, his theory was based on mathematical and psychological rather than neurological ideas—but in a flash, he suddenly saw that the picture could be interpreted as showing how the architecture of the brain agrees with his theory! This correspondence, though not strictly necessary to Kanerva's work, adds to it a certain degree of confirmation and sheer intellectual excitement that make it even more credible and tantalizing.

Sparse Distributed Memory began in 1974 as a paper written for a class on human memory given by Gordon Bower of Standford's psychology department. The main ideas were developed then, and in a couple of years they had been fleshed out, written up, and entitled simply "Kirja"—the Finnish word for "book". However, Pentti Kanerva is a perfectionist, and he was not quite satisfied with his work in that form, even though highly discriminating readers were very enthusiastic about it. He continued working on it until he felt all the bugs were out of it, and this is the finished product. Luckily, it has lost none of its freshness or originality. To be sure, there are other people who have been thinking along similar lines, which is reassuring. In may opinion, however, no one else has had as rich and clear a vision as Kanerva's (although some researchers have made related discoveries, confirming the plausibility of this approach).

Psychologists interested in memory should certainly be among this book's primary audience, of course, but neurologists would be no less apt. Then there are readers who could get something out of it purely on the mathematical side (Kanerva has found very interesting results on the properties of an important topological space). Finally, artificial-intelligence researchers will encounter in this book a new way of thinking about one of the central questions of their field: how associative memory could be implemented in a computer.

This book, because of its pristine mathematical beauty and its great clarity, excited me deeply when I read it, and I believe it will have the same effect on many others, whether they are professionals in the field of cognitive science or not. Before I came across it, I had read many articles describing intricate properties of neurons, the many varieties of neurotransmitters and second-messenger molecules, synaptic-modification processes, complex and hypercomplex cells, columns in the visual cortex, and so on.

All of this was fascinating but seemed very biological and microscopic: altogether quite distant from everyday mental experiences. I simply had never come across a cogent theory that addressed brain mechanisms on a global level. Pentti Kanerva's memory model was a revelation for me: it was the very first piece of research I had ever run across that made me feel I could glimpse the distant goal of understanding how the brain works as a whole. It gave me a concrete sense for how familiar mental phenomena could be thought of as distributed patterns of micro-events, thanks to beautiful mathematics. May Kanerva's "Kirja" in this, its polished form, be a similar mind-opener for many other readers!

Douglas R. Hofstadter
Psychology Department
University of Michigan

Preface

This book is the result of a thirty-year pursuit. Human memory has fascinated me since my college days, and I have wanted to understand it in a way that would allow the building of devices that function like human memory. May early interest in computers was motivated more by the desire to understand information-handling by the nervous system than by fast calculation. Even if the traditional uses of computers have dominated my professional life, that original interest was always there, affecting the way I looked at things. It has manifested itself in a mathematical model of human long-term memory that has surprising connections to conventional computer memories.

Henry W. Jensen, dean of Warren Wilson College in North Carolina and a professor of botany, was a major influence in my wanting to pursue a scientific career. He was my first teacher to admit openly that there were as yet unanswered questions in science and to teach accordingly. Many years later, at Stanford, Egon Loebner taught me in the same spirit about the processes of invention and discovery.

My early enthusiasm in neural-net models was nurtured in classes taught by Michael Arbib at Stanford in the late 1960s. I began to develop a mathematical theory of memory during Gordon Bower's class on human information processing at Stanford in the spring of 1974, and I described my model for the first time in a term paper for that class. Proving the model's mathematical validity then became the subject of my doctoral dissertation. I developed the proof on long hikes in Palo Alto's Foothills Park and wrote it down in the first draft of my dissertation in 1976 and 1977. The proof is statistical, and it uses methods I learned from Gustav Elfving at the University of Helsinki in the early 1960s. Further material was included in the final dissertation, which appeared in the spring of 1984 and was reproduced as a technical report by the Center for the Study of Language and Information at Stanford (Kanerva 1984). The first nine chapters and the appendixes of the present book are an edited version of the dissertation, and early ideas for chapter 10 have also appeared in print (Kanerva 1986).

I did my dissertation work in isolation, as the present boom in neural nets had not yet started and the previous one had long since ended. In fact, I assumed that people had given up on modeling of this kind, and I was concerned about my work's suitability for a dissertation. In the course of the work I developed my own geometric approach to the subject, and therefore I like to refer to the result as "my sparse-distributed-memory model" even though very similar models had already been proposed by David Marr and by James Albus in their doctoral dissertations. It also turns out that others, at disparate locations and with disparate backgrounds, were making fundamental discoveries about artificial neural systems through the 1960s and the 1970s: James Anderson at Brown, Stephen Grossberg at Boston University, Teuvo Kohonen in Finland, Bernard Widrow at Stanford, David Willshaw in England, et al.

Marr's work was brought to my attention by Douglas Hofstadter as he was reading the first draft of my dissertation. My discussion of the cerebellum had reminded him of Marr's model of the cerebellum, and he suggested that I look into it. I found our models to have much in common, and I was at the same time delighted and disappointed: delighted to find somebody who would understand my work, and disappointed at seeing footprints all over a terrain that I had assumed to be previously unexplored. I came to admire Marr's work, and although we talked only once—over the telephone—the interaction was significant. He asked me about the capacity of my model, and that resulted in my discussing memory capacity in the dissertation. Another thing I remember from our conversation was his reason for shifting the emphasis of his own research away from neural nets: He had concluded that neural machinery is extremely powerful and can perform just about any function, and that it was therefore most important to understand mathematically the tasks that an organism and its subsystems (e.g., vision) have to perform.

Much later I saw references to the Marr-Albus theory of the cerebellum, which led me to look into Albus's work. By then, Albus's book *Brains, Behavior, and Robotics* (1981) had been out for some time. In it I found the subject treated with unusual clarity and depth; the book is a constant inspiration to me. In discussions with Albus I learned that he had developed his theory independently of Marr, and indeed the details of his theory are unique.

In the 1980s the topic of artificial neural systems has become more popular than ever before—the field is exploding. I have included relatively little about this later development in the present book: only the architectures most closely related to mine and some general references. In essence, the book retains the flavor of my dissertation.

I wrote the introduction and chapters 1–9 as a graduate student at the Institute for Mathematical Studies in the Social Sciences at Stanford University, and chapter 10 as a postdoctoral fellow and visiting scholar at the

Center for the Study of Language and Information at Stanford and as a research scientist at the Research Institute for Advanced Computer Science at the NASA Ames Research Center. I am indebted to all these institutions and their people for providing the facilities and the atmosphere for the work. I am particularly indebted to Patrick Suppes, the director of the Institute for Mathematical Studies and my academic advisor in philosophy, for fostering a dissertation that at the time was quite foreign to philosophy and for providing a computer laboratory where I could truly learn about computers. The group of people there with whom I worked and from whom I learned is quite extraordinary: Dow Brian, Douglas Danforth, Scott Daniels, John Prebus, Michael Raugh, Ronald Roberts, and Brian Tolliver, to mention but a few. I am grateful to Jaakko Hintikka and John McCarthy for serving on my thesis committee.

As an unofficial reader, Douglas Hofstadter has been my most thorough critic—and the most encouraging. It is due largely to his influence, and Michael Raugh's, that I have been able to continue this research since completing my dissertation. Brian Tolliver and Lauri Kanerva helped me program the text editor with which I wrote the manuscript. Jon Barwise and John Perry gracefully took me on as a postdoctoral fellow. Their invaluable support came at what was a difficult time for me. In my present job I have benefited greatly from the interest that Peter Denning, Michael Flynn, Michael McGreevy, David Nagel, and others have shown in my work. In furthering the work, the people in our SDM research group at the Research Institute for Advanced Computer Science deserve a special mention: Ronald Chrisley, David Cohn, Douglas Danforth, Louis Jaeckel, Umesh Joglekar, James Keeler, Harrison Leong, Bruno Olshausen, Michael Raugh, David Rogers, and Avery Wang. Of my personal friends, Dikran Karagueuzian has followed this project the longest, encouraging me and eagerly awaiting the completion of the book. In finishing it I have had the unfaltering support and encouragement of Anne Kostick. Finally, Betty and Harry Stanton welcomed my effort and waited faithfully for the manuscript.

Several people have left their marks on the book directly. Dianne Kanerva edited the introduction and the first nine chapters and gave professional advice on the style and on all matters about writing. She also pointed out in the early stages that the memory equation I had come up with—and was a excited about—amounted to a pointer chain. Douglas Hofstadter gave thorough comments on the entire book, and Michael Raugh on chapter 10. The terms *hard location* and *autonomous learning system* were suggested to me by Louis Jaeckel, who also pointed out that the distribution of the third side of the triangle is related to the hypergeometric distribution and that the original table 7.1 was not quite right. Nancy Etchemendy drew the illustrations, and Paul Bethge at The MIT Press did the final editing.

My most sincere thanks to you all.

Very special thanks are due to my family. My wife, Dianne, and our sons, Kalle, Lauri, and Jonni, bore with me through my many years as a graduate student. They also shared in the development of the ideas expounded in this book. My parents, Yrjö and Helmi, have always been genuinely interested in whatever I was doing.

The completion of the manuscript was accompanied by a great personal tragedy, as my wife of thirty years died of cancer in 1986. Dianne was intelligent, perceptive, and giving of her self. She was excited by ideas, and she understood my work and the way I work. She also helped me professionally with her mastery of the English language, her publication expertise, and her delicate skill as an editor. May this book honor her memory among those whose lives she touched.

The research reported in this book was supported in part by NASA Cooperative Agreement NCC 2-408 with the Universities Space Research Association and by a gift from the System Development Foundation to the Center for the Study of Language and Information. Figure 9.2 is based on an illustration in the January 1975 issue of *Scientific American* (p. 58), with permission from W. H. Freeman and Company.

Sparse Distributed Memory

Introduction

As we live our lives, our brains accumulate a record of our experiences, and we make constant use of that record. By concentrating on something we can ensure its inclusion in the record, but many things are recorded without our paying attention to them. Likewise, retrieval of the record goes on without our necessarily being aware of it. Recognizing a face, recalling things that happened to us yesterday, singing a song, and carrying out a practiced athletic performance mean retrieving and making use of parts of the record.

In this study of memory I seek answers to two questions: (1) how to organize the record so that it will be retrieved in the right way under the right circumstances—that is, in a way that agrees with how people distinguish the familiar from the unfamiliar and how they recall past events—and (2) how to construct, from neuronlike components, a physical memory that allows for the proper storage and retrieval of the record. I will use the word *record* to mean a sequence of memory items that represents the experiences of a person—a film or tape of one's life—and the word *memory* to mean the medium for the storage of the record—a tangible, concrete thing.

A few examples will illustrate the aspects of memory that I wish to capture with the theory and demonstrate with the model. First, how are concepts related to one another? If we try to imagine all the concepts we have in our heads, we might say that any one concept is unrelated to most of the rest; however, for any two unrelated concepts we can always find an intermediate concept that is related to each of the first two.

Many things can serve to link concepts: looks (the letter o looks like a circle), frequent coincidence (rain and winter in California), category (birds and bees are animals that fly), and so forth. In the following riddle, links between unrelated concepts are made with words that sound alike:

> Why are fire engines painted red?
> Firemen's suspenders are red, too.
> Two and two are four.
> Four times three is twelve.

Twelve inches in a foot.
A foot is a ruler.
Queen Mary was a ruler.
Queen Mary sailed the sea.
The sea has sharks.
Sharks have fins.
The Russians conquered the Finns.
The Russians' color is red.
Fire engines are always rushin'.
So that's why they're painted red!

Although we normally ignore such links, they are there, and they can tell us something about the mathematical space for memory items. Translated into a requirement for the model, memory items should be arranged in such a way that most items are unrelated to one another but most pairs of items can be linked by just one or two intermediate items. This requirement affects the choice of the mathematical space for memory items, also called the semantic space.

Furthermore, many links come about automatically rather than being learned explicitly by exposure to them. A person need only be a speaker of English to "understand" the fire-engine riddle even when hearing or seeing it for the first time. In other words, *some links (i.e., associations) are learned, but others are a property of the mathematical space for memory items.*

How easily old information is recovered can give an idea of how the memory is organized. If we are shown a photograph of a face and are asked to name the person, our subjective experience is usually one of the following: We recognize the person immediately and readily come up with the name; or we recognize the person but struggle with the name; or the face looks familiar but we feel uncertain; or, finally, we can tell immediately that we have never known the person. This last thing is most likely to happen if there is something unusual about the face and the person is truly unknown to us.

I shall elaborate on two things about this example: first, that sometimes we are immediately sure that we do or do not know the person in the picture; second, that when we are not sure, we have a sense about our uncertainty and can guess quite well how close to having the answer we are. The first of these has been referred to as knowing that one knows and the second as the tip-of-the-tongue phenomenon.

That we can know immediately whether we know the person tells us that we do not scan through the entire record sequentially until we find a match but, rather, that we reach for the relevant parts of the record directly. In some sense, then, the search cue—the picture of the face—serves as an *address* to memory, and we need only to find out whether the addressed part has information stored in it. If not, we report that the cue is new or unknown to us.

Accordingly, in my theory, *patterns serve as addresses to memory*—and not just previously encountered patterns, but new patterns as well. In other words, the memory has a permanent addressing framework that is independent of what we have learned so far, and the record is stored in and retrieved from the addressed parts of the memory. Seeing a picture of an unusual face means, then, that the address pattern is unusual or unique. Therefore, the addressed parts of the memory are unique to that face and will not have much information in them that would interfere with the recognition of the face, and this makes it possible for us to decide quickly whether we know the person.

Recall can be striking and quite unexpected. A unique cue, such as a special sound or smell, can recreate an old event in a flash. The smell of bread baking in an oven can bring vivid memories of Grandmother's kitchen, a scene that we may not have entertained for decades. This is sometimes taken to mean that we never forget what we have once learned and that all we need in order to retrieve it is the right cue. However, it is well known that similar experiences do affect the later recall of these experiences (this is referred to in psychology as proactive and retroactive interference). Accordingly, in constructing a memory model I am assuming that memory capacity is limited, that items stored in the memory interact with one another, and that this interaction affects recall.

Fundamental to the model are the storage and retrieval of *sequences*, that is, memory items for events that occur one after another in time. A person's life record is one long sequence that grows while the person lives. Acquiring skills, in particular, involves the learning of sequences.

Music, language, physical tasks (the use of our muscles), and dreams all require sequential retrieval of parts of the record. One item in the sequence helps to retrieve others, particularly those that come soon after it in the sequence. Recalling the letters of the alphabet is a good example. It is by far easiest for us to recite the letters in alphabetical order. If asked to give every third letter, we most likely retrieve the whole list but say out loud only every third letter. But if asked to give the alphabet in reverse, most of us would be at a loss. So here is something that we have learned in a certain order and then most easily retrieve in that same order, with one item in the list proving to be an excellent cue for the next.

A remarkable property of memory is that we are able to find a stored sequence on the basis of some part of it and then to follow the sequence from that point on. A few bars of a melody, from nearly anywhere in a familiar song, need first by recognized as bars of music and not as mere random noise, but from there on we can hum the rest of the tune. In computer terminology, we can address into any part of the stored record directly (random access), and we can also read the record in sequence (sequential access). Providing for both in a natural way is a key element of my memory model.

My wanting to construct the model from neuronlike components comes from the desire to find a *physiologically plausible* theory. This has had an unexpected payoff even in the course of this study: As the architecture for the memory became evident to me, I was struck by its resemblance to the structure of the cortex of the cerebellum. That correspondence is described near the end of the book.

The discussion above gives the psychological and physiological motivation for this study in rather general terms. The theory itself is abstract and the model is an idealization, and both deal only with limited aspects of the real phenomena of memory. But they do provide a framework for the discussion of some basic issues. For example, it makes sense to ask, within this framework, whether human memory is content-addressable or what might it mean to say that it is associative; and these issues are discussed in the book.

In the model, memory items are represented by n-bit words, with n in the range 100–10,000. The bits of a word are thought of as abstract features. How the coding of information into this form might be accomplished is discussed at the end of the book.

This introduction gives background and indicates the approach that I will take. Also, the premises of the work are given here.

Chapters 1–3 are about foundations. A reader with a sufficient background in mathematics, computers, and neuron models can move directly to the last section of chapter 3, which is a criticism of learning models that appeal to the Perceptron Convergence Theorem. Chapter 1 introduces the mathematics used in the study. The main tools are the binomial and normal distributions. I assume that the reader knows the elements of probability theory. Set notation is used throughout, but not much of set theory. All in all, the mathematics is rather elementary; however, there is a fair amount of it, as fits the nature of the work.

Basic facts about the random-access memory of a computer are laid out in chapter 2. Some principles of computer-memory architecture are also discussed there. Chapter 3 reviews certain properties of neurons and gives a mathematical abstraction based on them: the linear threshold function. In the rest of the book, *neuron* refers to this abstraction.

After these preliminaries I give a new interpretation of neuron function, that of *address decoding*. It is contained in chapter 4, and it constitutes the first major insight of this study. A linear threshold function—a neuron—is a pattern-matching device for a set of patterns centered around a specific pattern, called the neuron's *address*. In fact, address decoding in a conventional computer memory is a special case of address decoding by a neuron. In chapter 5 I describe a machine, which I call the Best-Match Machine, that makes use of the address-decoder neurons to solve a problem that is difficult for a conventional computer. The further development of the memory model is based on this solution.

Chapters 6 and 7 deal with the practical problems of building a memory with an enormous address space (e.g., $2^{1,000}$ addresses) without requiring an enormous number of storage locations. We will see that a small random sample (2^{20}) of storage locations drawn from the potential 2^{1000} will perform the memory function if copies of each item are stored in many locations. *The mathematical feasibility of this distributed, sparse memory is the main result of this study.*

The formal properties of the model that correspond to knowing that one knows and to the tip-of-the-tongue state are discussed at the end of chapter 7.

Chapter 8 deals with learning. The experience of an organism is represented by a sequence of n-bit words and modeled by Markov chains. The problem I discuss is that of what to store in memory, and where, so that it can be retrieved when needed. The unifying idea of the theory is that *there is no fundamental distinction between addresses to memory and the data stored in the storage locations; the data stored in memory are addresses to the memory.* To allow sequential retrieval, the data are stored as a pointer chain (a linked list) in a generalized random-access memory. The k-fold Markov chain is introduced as a special case of the kth-order Markov chain. It is particularly well suited for storage in a sparse distributed memory.

In chapter 9 I show how to build a sparse distributed memory from neuronlike components. The solution suggests a method of storing the data: A storage location can be realized as a set of n counters, one for each bit position. The resulting structure is surprisingly similar to structures found in the cortex of the cerebellum, which suggests that the cerebellar cortex quite literally is a random-access memory. This interpretation of the cerebellar cortex is the third major result of this study.

The final chapter, chapter 10, is about autonomous learning systems, human beings and animals being our prime examples of such systems. How might such systems be organized, and what role in their organization would be played by a sparse distributed memory? The key ideas in the chapter are that these systems base their operation on an internal model of the world, which they build through experience, and that a sparse distributed memory is ideal for storing a predictive model of the world. The fundamental role of sensory encoding is also discussed.

Perspective

Throughout the book I make reference to the computer, a most complex and versatile human invention and one designed exclusively for the processing of information. It serves as a model, a physical entity that we know how to construct and hence believe we can understand. However, in solving practical problems, such as those of massive computation, we create objects the essence of which can escape our notice for a long time. This appears to be true of the computer, for the study reveals that the architectures of ordinary computer memory and sparse distributed memory are basically the same.

When I first learned about computers, about thirty years ago, I was intrigued. What really interested me was whether understanding them could help us understand how we ourselves work.

My first surprise and disappointment with computers came from realizing that all that circuitry was executing just one primitive instruction at a time. I was soon advised that it did not matter. Anything that is effectively computable can be programmed on a computer. Early theoretical work on computability had established this with the simplest of models for the computer, the Turing machine.

But in real life it does matter; the architecture of the computer and the organization of computation determine what the computer is good for. For example, computers can be used to gather and analyze data and to respond to changes in the environment in real time. In so doing they serve a function similar to that of the nervous system and operate under similar time constraints. It is therefore reasonable to expect that some structures for carrying out computation in computers might also work well in the nervous system.

Ultimately, we want to understand learning. We could try to find out how information is processed and stored by the nervous system. That would call for careful physiological analysis. But when a system is sufficiently complex and very general, as are computers and even more so the central nervous system, it is almost impossible to infer function from even the most detailed description of the structure. At best, we can suggest possible functions for a given structure. In fact, there usually comes a point beyond which further analysis of the structure contributes nothing to the understanding of the function but tells only how the function is realized in that particular instance. For example, the logical 'and' function of a computer can be realized with switches operated by relays, with vacuum tubes, or with transistors. A computer-logic designer does not have to know the physics of transistors to design with components based on transistors. So, something in addition to structural analysis is needed.

In trying to understand a complex entity it is useful to try to determine its function and to analyze its structure at the same time; either provides a check for the other. However, the initial emphasis might be on understanding the function. In repairing a faulty structure (the criterion of faulty usually being that there is an impaired function!), we try first to understand the function of whatever we need to fix. Our standard questions are: What is it supposed to do? Under what conditions? How would I have designed the thing in the first place? Underlying such questions is the belief that an object with such and such a function can be constructed reasonably in only a limited number of ways. A fool would deny the existence of such limits, a novice is ignorant of them, a professional will readily assess them and tell you what they are because he knows what is possible, and a genius can see beyond such limits.

So we should try to imagine what mechanisms could support the information processing implicit in animal and human behavior, and we should then use anatomical and physiological data to check the feasibility of our hypotheses. May favorite example of scientific progress in this vein is the discovery of the laws of heredity by Mendel in the mid-1800s. Without the aid of a microscope, Mendel "saw" what the hereditary mechanisms are like. I can imagine him saying: "Fellow scientists, when you someday develop adequate instruments to see what is going on, look for particles that normally occur in pairs but separate before pollination." Mendel's theory of heredity started as a mathematical theory; only later did observation make it into a physical theory.

Physiological data, in turn, can inspire new hypotheses, which then need to be checked for their mathematical adequacy. For example, the existence of excitatory and inhibitory neurons throughout the nervous system and the summing of inputs by neurons have inspired the idea that changes in synaptic conductivity are the primary vehicle of memory and learning. But we need definitive models (beyond the perceptron, discussed in chapter 3) that will be based on this assumption. It is inevitable that something in the nervous system must change to accommodate learning, but we need a clear idea of what that something could be. Here, thorough mathematical analysis is a powerful method for suggesting good candidates and for weeding out unlikely ones.

I shall examine the usefulness of two ideas about computers in developing a theory of memory: the suitability of the neuron as a building block for the random-access memory of a computer, and the suitability of a random-access memory as a model for the long-term memory of a human.

Background

In their article on anatomy, the authors of the first *Encyclopaedia Britannica* (1771) wrote about the brain thus:

Uses of the Brain and its Appendages in general.
Malphighi was the first who discovered the brain to be a gland, or an organ fitted to separate some particular fluid from the mass of blood.

The infinite number of small secretory clusters strain or filter the mass of blood carried to them by the numerous ramifications, and separate from it an excessively fine fluid; the remaining blood being conveyed back by the same number of venal extremities, into the sinuses of the dura matter, and from thence into the jugular and vertebral veins.

This subtle fluid, commonly called *animal spirit, nervous juice,* or *liquor of the nerves,* is continually forced into the medullary fibres of the white portion of the cerebrum, cerebellum, medulla oblongata, and medulla spinalis; and by the intervention of these fibres supplies and fills the nerves, which are a continuation of them. (p. 288)

By that time the gross anatomy of the nervous system was known.

The anatomy and physiology of the nervous system have been studied in greater and greater detail in the last 200 years. In the early 1900s, however, it was still commonly believed that the nerves formed a continuous network in the sense that signals passed continuously along the nerve fibers and from one fiber to another.

Sound theoretical work on the functioning of the nervous system became possible only after the synaptic theory of signal transmission was adopted. According to this theory, signals are transmitted from one neuron to the next across synapses, some of which are excitatory and others inhibitory. Transmission across an excitatory synapse increases the next neuron's tendency to fire, and transmission across an inhibitory synapse decreases that tendency. I will comment briefly on the work of three people who in the 1940s based their theoretical work on these ideas: McCulloch and Pitts (1943) and Hebb (1949). McCulloch and Pitts considered the neuron as a logic module for computation; Hebb, who focused on the cell assembly, formulated structures that could support psychological phenomena.

McCulloch and Pitts described the Boolean functions (e.g., logical 'and', logical 'or', logical 'not') that neurons could perform. It is a fact of mathematical logic that all Boolean functions with any number of arguments can be constructed from these simple functions of at most two arguments. The obvious conclusion is that any desired network can be built from neuron-like components. This has been taken as a confirmation of the notion that neurons, with their synapses, are the basic computational components of the nervous system. Later work by Minsky (1954) reinforces this view by demonstrating the necessity of both excitatory and inhibitory synapses (or their equivalents) to the realization of the Boolean functions.

Hebb tried to fill the gap between physiological data and psychological phenomena. In his theory, groups of cells become assigned to particular tasks. The goals of the theory are comprehensive, but the details are lacking by today's standards.

The element missing in Hebb's work is a rigorous and sufficiently rich notion of computation. Consequently, the cell-assembly theory fails to suggest adequate mechanisms for the processing and storage of information. This should not be too surprising; the theories of automata and computation were then unknown even to most mathematicians, and computers, as we know them now, barely existed. However, elements of Hebb's theory are found in much of the subsequent work of others.

In the 1950s, von Neumann (1951, 1952) became interested in the logic behind the construction of the nervous system. He compared the numbers and types of components of a computer to those of the brain. His writings present, in a most lucid way, the aspects of the nervous system that seem important to a mathematician trying to understand the processing of information by the brain. For example, he emphasized the digital (all-or-none) nature of the neuron signal. As a prominent mathematician and one of the pioneers of the stored-program computer (even today, the digital computer is known as the von Neumann machine), he was one of the first people with sufficient background in the theory of computing and computer architecture to develop a comprehensive theory of information processing by the brain. He died in 1957 without having proposed such a theory, but his book *The Computer and the Brain*, published in 1958, indicates the extent of his interest in the subject.

In the late 1950s and the 1960s, theoretical work was done on neural-net models that conform to a general plan but do not specify connections in detail. Rosenblatt (1958, 1962) introduced a neural-circuit model called the *perceptron* and demonstrated its ability to learn to recognize patterns. His work, like Hebb's, inspired many others. (For a commentary on the work on perceptrons, see Block 1970.)

The first comprehensive memory models that follow Hebb's ideas appeared in the late 1960s and the early 1970s. Brindley (1969) proposed a mathematical model of learning in neural nets via the modification of synapses, and the remarkable work of Marr (1969, 1970, 1971) and of Albus (1971) resulted in theories for several kinds of cortex found in the brain.

In Marr's theory, memory events are identified with the states of sets of fibers (the firing states of neurons as transmitted along their axons). Time is discrete, and at any moment an individual fiber is either active (on) or inactive (off). One set of inputs to the memory is provided by input fibers (mossy fibers in the cerebellum; see figures 9.2 and 9.3 below) sampled by codon cells (granule cells in the cerebellum), with each codon cell permanently set to sample from three to five input fibers. If at a given moment the number of active input fibers in the sample exceeds a threshold, the codon cell becomes active (it fires); otherwise, it is inactive. For example, a codon cell with four inputs could fire when any three or all four of its inputs are active. The activation pattern of the codon cells corresponding to the activation pattern of the input fibers (the input pattern) is called the *codon representation* of the input pattern.

When the codon cells are constructed properly, the codon representations of two input patterns overlap much less than do the input patterns themselves. The overlapping of patterns is measured by comparing the set of active fibers (or firing cells) common to both patterns with the set of fibers active (or cells firing) in at least one of the patterns. (The size of the intersection of active fibers, or firing cells, is divided by the size of their union.) The codon representation thus exaggerates the differences between patterns.

At the next stage, the codon-cell outputs (parallel fibers in the cerebellum) are sampled by an array of cells (Purkinje cells in the cerebellum) that provide the output of the memory. The synapses made by the codon-cell axons with the output-cell dendrites are modifiable, and the output of each output cell is a linear threshold function of its inputs. The states of the output cells at a given time constitute the memory's output pattern at that time.

The output patterns to be associated with the input patterns are presented to the memory along a second set of input fibers (climbing fibers in the cerebellum) that go directly to the output cells. Concurrent activity along these input fibers and the codon-cell axons modifies the synapses made by the codon-cell axons with the output-cell dendrites, constituting writing into memory.

Marr proves an important convergence property about his model: When a number of associations have been stored in memory (an association is a pair of patterns, the first of which is an input to memory and the second of which is the desired output associated with that input) and a new input pattern is presented that resembles a stored input, the output from the memory is a pattern that resembles the stored associated output more closely than the new input pattern resembles the stored input. Here, as above, the resemblance of two patterns is the relative size of the overlap of the two patterns. For this convergence to take place, the number of stored associations must be below a certain limit, and the new input pattern must be sufficiently close to the closest stored input pattern. (The more associations stored, the closer the two input patterns have to be for the output patterns to converge.)

Applied to the cerebellar cortex, Marr's theory assumes that the synapses made by the parallel fibers with the Purkinje-cell dendrites are modifiable. Experimental evidence of this has been reported by Ito (1982).

Marr's theory goes beyond what I have just described. In addition to the cerebellum, Marr has interpreted other structures found in the brain.

A mathematical model of the cerebellum similar to Marr's was developed independently by Albus (1971, 1975, 1981). Their models and my sparse distributed memory are alike in that they have—in terms introduced more recently—a *hidden layer with fixed coefficients that maps input patterns to subsets of storage locations*. The storage and retrieval of a pattern then takes place in the currently active subset, with most of the locations inactive at any one time. This is in contrast to multilayered back-propagation networks, in which the coefficients of all layers are subject to learning and in which, for any given input pattern, all units of the hidden layer are active to varying degrees instead of being just on or off (see, e.g., Rumelhart et al. 1986; Sejnowski and Rosenberg 1987).

Characteristic of the memory models above is that a stored pattern is *distributed* over many locations of memory, with a single location partaking in the storage of many different patterns, and that retrieval is by mathematical *reconstruction* from the contents of many locations. Such distributed representation is typical of most models of associative memory. Some of the earlier ones, with lesser resemblance to my model, have been described by Aleksander (1970), Aleksander and Stonham (1979), Anderson (1968, 1970, 1977, 1983), Grossberg (1983—this is a collection of Grossberg's papers originally published between 1968 and 1980), Hinton et al. (1984), Hopfield (1982), Kohonen (1972, 1977, 1984), Widrow (1962), Willshaw (1981), and Willshaw and Longuet-Higgins (1970).

In addition to the distributed models, *localized* models have been proposed as models of human memory. A single memory location or node of a localized model is associated with a single stored pattern or concept. Of such models, Baum, Moody, and Wilczek's (1986) sparse memory that creates a "grandmother" cell for each stored pattern is in some ways similar to my sparse distributed memory, whereas the semantic-net models of Feldman and Ballard (1982) are entirely different.

An excellent overview of the early models has been given by Anderson and Hinton (1981); for an important two-volume collection of more recent works, see Rumelhart and McClelland 1986 and McClelland and Rumelhart 1986.

Common to all of these models is that they can operate with imprecise and incomplete data and can construct from those data the most likely associated patterns. Therefore, they are all sensitive to similarity. Furthermore, the distributed models in particular are rather immune to hardware failures. According to these models, speed is obtained by making the circuits very large and doing many computations at once (that is, in parallel).

Since processing is highly distributed, these models require only a simple centralized executive.

The distributed models of memory may be contrasted with common data structures programmed for ordinary computer memories, which are all localized. The requirements for the programmed data structures are much like those for human memory: to allow reliable and timely retrieval and updating of information stored in memory. However, the organization of the memory is totally different.

A computer memory can be organized into arrays, records, trees, lists, stacks, and the like, and many different methods of storing and finding information in them are used. The methods that will be discussed here are hash coding, linked lists, and trie memory.

Hash coding is a method of mapping—with a hashing function—a *sparse* set of points (e.g., a set of finite sequences, such as vocabulary words) into a target space, which is usually a linear or two-dimensional array of memory locations. The goals of hash coding are (1) to store the sparse set in a small space, (2) to answer quickly the question of whether a test element is a member of the stored set, and (3) to find quickly the information associated with a stored element.

Hashing functions are never one-to-one; so if a test element is mapped into an occupied location of memory, it does not necessarily mean that the test element is in the stored set. To find out whether it is, the test element must be compared with the stored element or elements that hash into that same location. (The need for such a comparison is avoided by the method called trie memory, which is discussed below.)

A good hashing function fills the target space uniformly, regardless of any clustering in the stored set. Functions that yield random points of the target space are therefore good hashing functions. Consequently, hash coding destroys any structure that the stored set may have, so it is a poor model of human memory.

Linked lists provide a method of mapping *sequences* of unknown length into a linear array of memory locations. The nth element of a sequence is accessed by starting from the head of the list and tracing over the $n - 1$ intervening links. This method of storage can serve as a model of human memory for storing sequences, in the sense that one element in the sequence serves to retrieve the next element. The idea of a linked list is fundamental to the model of memory developed in the present book.

A *set of sequences* can be stored in a memory structure called *trie memory* (Fredkin 1960). A trie memory is a mapping of finite sequences of objects (symbols) into unique memory locations. The objects are elements of a small, finite set. For example, the objects could be letters of the alphabet, and the sequences could be vocabulary words. Two of the goals are the same as with hash-coded memory: a quick answer to the question of whether a test sequence is among the stored sequences and a quick way to find the information associated with a stored sequence.

A set of sequences is stored in a trie memory by building a tree, the nodes of which correspond, one to one, to the initial subsequences of the stored set. The terminal nodes then correspond to the complete sequences of the stored set. Addressing a trie memory with a test sequence means traversing the tree to find out whether the process ends at a terminal node. If it does, the test sequence is among the stored sequences, and the information associated with the stored sequence is found at the terminal node.

Trie memory is a distant relative of the memory model developed herein. The kinship is seen in how the memory is addressed at each node of the tree: The next symbol in the sequence—the encoding of the next symbol—serves as an address of the next node. (In a trie memory, this address is relative to the present node.)

A trie memory behaves very unlike the memory model of the present study when the memory is addressed with sequences that are very similar to one another. Assume that two sequences differ in only one place. If this place is at or near the beginnings of the sequences, the two sequences are mapped very far from each other in a trie memory; if it is at or near the ends of the sequences, they are mapped very close to each other. This is a simple consequence of a trie memory's being a tree. Just the opposite is true in the memory model of the present study: The more distant the past, the less relevant it is to where in the memory the present symbol (and the sequence ending in that symbol) is mapped.

Common to all these methods of addressing computer memory is that they work well only if the retrieval cue is *identical* to a cue (an address) with which information has been stored. None of them is designed to find information when the retrieval cue is similar but not identical to an address used in storing information. In that sense, none of them is a good model of human memory.

Premises

We are still far from understanding how the brain works, and I believe that an adequate theory must take into account all aspects of the phenomenon: anatomy, engineering, mathematics (computation theory), physiology, and psychology—listed here in alphabetical order. I will approach the topic mathematically, attending to the requirements of computer engineering and architecture.

The aspect of the human (and animal) experience that I try to understand with my theory of memory is the retrieval of information about the past, both "at random" (i.e., directly from any part of the memory) and in sequence. The theory is developed with reference to a very simple space—

that of n-tuples of zeros and ones—and is based on the following four ideas:

1. The space $\{0, 1\}^n$, for large n ($100 < n < 10{,}000$), has properties that correspond to some of our intuitive notions about the relationships between concepts, and so it seems appropriate to represent memory items as points of the space $\{0, 1\}^n$. The data that are stored and retrieved can be thought of as n-component patterns of zeros and ones.
2. Neurons with n inputs are ideal as address decoders of a random-access memory with the address space $\{0, 1\}^n$.
3. The unifying principle: The address space and the datum space are the same. The data stored in memory are addresses to the memory.
4. Time is included in the memory trace by virtue of where in the memory the data are stored.

Symbols

For a list of the symbols used in the book, see appendix E.

Chapter 1
Mathematical Foundations

The Space $\{0, 1\}^n$

The chief objects of study are n-dimensional vectors with binary components. Depending on the context, the vectors are called points, patterns, addresses, words, memory items, data, or events. This chapter is mostly about the properties of the vector space.

Let n be the number of dimensions of the space. The number of points, or possible memory items, is then 2^n. I will denote this number by N and will use N and 2^n to stand also for the space itself. (This usage is in accord with the von Neumann theory of ordinals, which defines a non-negative integer as the set of integers smaller than itself: $0 = \{\ \}$ and, for $i > 0$, $i = \{0, 1, 2, \ldots, i - 1\}$).

Points of N are naturally represented by n-tuples of zeros and ones (e.g., $\langle 0, 1, 0, 1, 1\rangle$) and can be written as n-bit integers in binary representation (01011). Thinking of them as integers, however, is misleading, since the integers are an ordered, one-dimensional set, whereas in the present context we have no reason to say that 00001, for example, does or does not come before 00100. The useful properties of the space $\{0, 1\}^n$ result from its large number of dimensions.

The space N together with the operations of coordinatewise (bitwise) 'and' and 'or' form a Boolean algebra. In this study we are concerned primarily with the *distances* between the points of N, or what will be called the *distribution* of N. A fuller characterization of the space than is given here can be found in Blumenthal and Menger 1970.

Concepts Related to the Space $\{0, 1\}^n$

Origin, 0 The point with all coordinates 0 is called the origin, $0 = 000\ldots00$.

Complement, 'x The complement, or *opposite*, of point x is the n-tuple that has ones where x has zeros and vice versa.

Norm, |x| The norm of point x is the number of ones in its binary representation.

Difference, x − y The difference of two points x and y is the n-tuple that has ones where x and y differ and zeros elsewhere. It is the bitwise 'exclusive or' of x and y: $x - y = x \oplus y$. The difference commutes: $x - y = y - x$.

Distance, d(x, y) The distance between two points x and y is the number of dimensions at which x and y differ. It is called the *Hamming distance* (its square root is the Euclidean distance) and is expressed in *bits*. Distance is the norm of the difference:

$$d(x, y) = |x - y|$$
$$= |x_0 - y_0| + \cdots + |x_{n-1} - y_{n-1}|.$$

Two points of N that are close to each other are said to be *similar*; that term is used mostly in a relative sense, as in "x is the element of X most similar to y."

Betweenness, x:y:z Point y is between points x and z if and only if the distance from x to z is the sum of the distances from x to y and from y to z; that is,

$$d(x, z) = d(x, y) + d(y, z).$$

It is easily seen that every bit of a point in between is a copy of the corresponding bit of an endpoint:

$x:y:z$ iff $y_i = x_i$ or $y_i = z_i$ for $i = 0, \ldots, n - 1$.

The relation $w:x:y:z:\ldots$ is defined recursively as $w:x:y$ & $x:y:z:\ldots$. Betweenness is symmetric ($x:y:z:\ldots$ iff $\ldots:z:y:x$) but not transitive (in the sense that $w:x:y:z$ does not imply $w:x:z$). Set Y is between points x and z ($x:Y:z$) if and only if all its points are between x and z. All of N is between a point and its complement: $x:N:`x$.

Orthogonality, x ⊥ y Point x is orthogonal to point y, or the two are *perpendicular* or *indifferent*, if and only if the distance between the two is half the number of dimensions:

$$d(x, y) = n/2.$$

The distance $n/2$ is called the *indifference distance* of $\{0, 1\}^n$. If x is orthogonal to y, it is also orthogonal to its complement $`y$ ($x$ is halfway between $y$ and $`y$): $x \perp y$ implies $x \perp `y$.

Circle, $O(r, x)$ A circle with radius r and center x is the set of points that are at most r bits from x:

$$O(r, x) = \{y \mid d(x, y) \leq r\}.$$

Any circle with radius n is the whole space N:

$$O(n, x) = N.$$

Examples   A small number of dimensions suffices to demonstrate these concepts. Let $n = 5$, $x = 00111$, and $y = 01010$. Then

Complement: $`x = 11000$, and $`y = 10101$.

Norm: $|x| = 3$, and $|y| = 2$.

Difference: $x - y = y - x = x \oplus y = 01101$ $(= `x - `y)$.

Distance: $d(x, y) = |x - y| = |01101| = 3$.

Betweenness: Any $z = 0^{**}1^*$, where each * is either 0 or 1, is between x and y. For example, $x:01110:y$.

Orthogonality: No point can be (exactly) orthogonal to x, because n is odd. $0101 \perp 0011$.

Circle: $O(1, x) = \{00111, 10111, 01111, 00011, 00101, 00110\}$.

The space N can be represented by the vertices of the unit cube in n-dimensional Euclidean space. The distance between two points of N is then the length of the shortest path along the edges of the cube joining the two points, also called the city-block distance. When two points are farther than one bit from each other, there are multiple shortest paths between them.

The Sphere Analogy   The vertices of an n-dimensional unit cube lie on the surface of an n-dimensional sphere with (Euclidean-metric) radius $\sqrt{n}/2$. This gives rise to the sphere analogy. I will call a space *spherical* if (1) any point x has a unique opposite $`x$, (2) the entire space is between any point $x$ and its opposite $`x$, and (3) all points are "equal" (meaning that for any two points x and y there is a distance-preserving automorphism of the space that maps x to y, so that from any of its points the space "looks" the same). The surface of a sphere (in Euclidean 3-space) clearly is spherical. According to the definition, N is also spherical, since $y \oplus x \oplus (\cdots)$ is an automorphism that maps x to y (in fact, for each of the $n!$ permutations of the coordinates there is an automorphism that maps x to y).

Because N is spherical, I have found it helpful to think of it as the surface of a sphere with circumference $2n$. All points of N are equally qualified as points of origin, and a point and its complement are like two poles at distance n from each other, with the entire space in between. The points halfway between the poles and perpendicular to them are like the equator. True to the sphere analogy, I refer to a set of points within a given distance from a point as a circle on N.

In addition to N's having a finite number of points and a sphere's being continuous, the spaces differ in other important ways. For example, the points of N between two points x and y are a $d(x,y)$-dimensional subspace of N, whereas the corresponding set on a sphere is a "straight" line (a segment of a great circle), unless y is the opposite of x, in which case it is the entire sphere. The segments (i.e., the minimal paths between two points) of N are not even unique. Also, the circles on N, as a rule, are not convex, as is shown by the following example: 00001 and 00010 are in the circle $O(1, 00000)$, and 00011 is between them but is not in the circle.

Some Properties of the Space $\{0, 1\}^n$

Because N is spherical in the sense defined above, it can be so "rotated" as to move any of its points to the origin. Therefore, in speaking of an arbitrary point x, it is often convenient to think of x as the origin, $x = 0$, because the distance from 0 to some other point y is simply the number of ones in y:

$$d(0, y) = |y - 0| = |y|.$$

Distribution of the Space N The number of points that are exactly d bits from an arbitrary point x (say, from the point 0) is the number of ways to choose d coordinates from a total of n coordinates, and is therefore given by the binomial coefficient

$$(n : d) = \binom{n}{d} = \frac{n!}{d!(n-d)!}.$$

The distribution of N thus is the binomial distribution with parameters n and p, where $p = \frac{1}{2}$. The mean of the binomial is $n/2$, and the variance is $n/4$. This distribution function will be denoted by $N(d)$. The normal distribution F with mean $n/2$ and standard deviation $\sqrt{n/2}$ is a good approximation to it:

$$N(d) = \Pr\{d(x, y) \leq d\}$$
$$\cong F\{(d - n/2)/\sqrt{n/4}\}.$$

Many properties of N will be derived below from the binomial distribution and its normal approximation.

Tendency to Orthogonality An outstanding property of N is that most of it lies at approximately the mean (indifference) distance $n/2$ from a point (and its complement), with only a minute fraction closer by or farther away. In other words, *most of the space is nearly orthogonal to any given point*, and the larger n is, the more pronounced is this effect. In terms of the sphere analogy, with any point and its complement taken as poles, almost all the space lies at or near the equator (as do the points of an n-dimensional Euclidean sphere).

The mathematics of it works out as follows: If we divide the mean distance $n/2$ by the standard deviation of distance $\sqrt{n}/2$, we get that the distance from a point to the bulk of the space (from a pole to the equator) is $\sqrt{n}$ standard deviations. For $n = 1{,}000$ it is 31.6 standard deviations. According to the normal distribution, over 0.999999 of the space lies within 5 standard deviations of the mean or within $(\sqrt{n} \pm 5)$ standard deviations from a point of N. With $n = 1{,}000$, the mean distance is 500 bits, but only about a millionth of the space is closer to the point than 422 bits or farther from it than 578 bits (5 standard deviations come to 78 bits). Some basic facts about the distribution of N are summarized in table 1.1 for $n = 100$, 1,000, and 10,000, and they also appear in figure 1.1.

The Third Side of a Triangle This subsection serves the next one, in which we are concerned with the distribution of points of a circle.

Three points of N define a triangle. What is the length of one side when the lengths of the other two are known? Let the known lengths be a and b,

Table 1.1
Distribution of the space N ($N = \{0, 1\}^n$).

Portion of the space N in range R about the mean distance	Number of dimensions, n					
	$n = 100$		$n = 1{,}000$		$n = 10{,}000$	
	Range R Bits	% of n	Range R Bits	% of n	Range R Bits	% of n
0.5	50 ± 3	6	500 ± 11	2	5,000 ± 34	0.6
0.98	50 ± 12	24	500 ± 37	7	5,000 ± 116	2.3
0.998	50 ± 15	30	500 ± 49	10	5,000 ± 154	3.1
0.9998	50 ± 19	38	500 ± 59	12	5,000 ± 186	3.7
0.999998	50 ± 24	48	500 ± 75	15	5,000 ± 238	4.8
0.999999998	50 ± 30	60	500 ± 95	19	5,000 ± 300	6.0
Mean distance	50		500		5,000	
Standard deviation of distance	5		15.8		50	

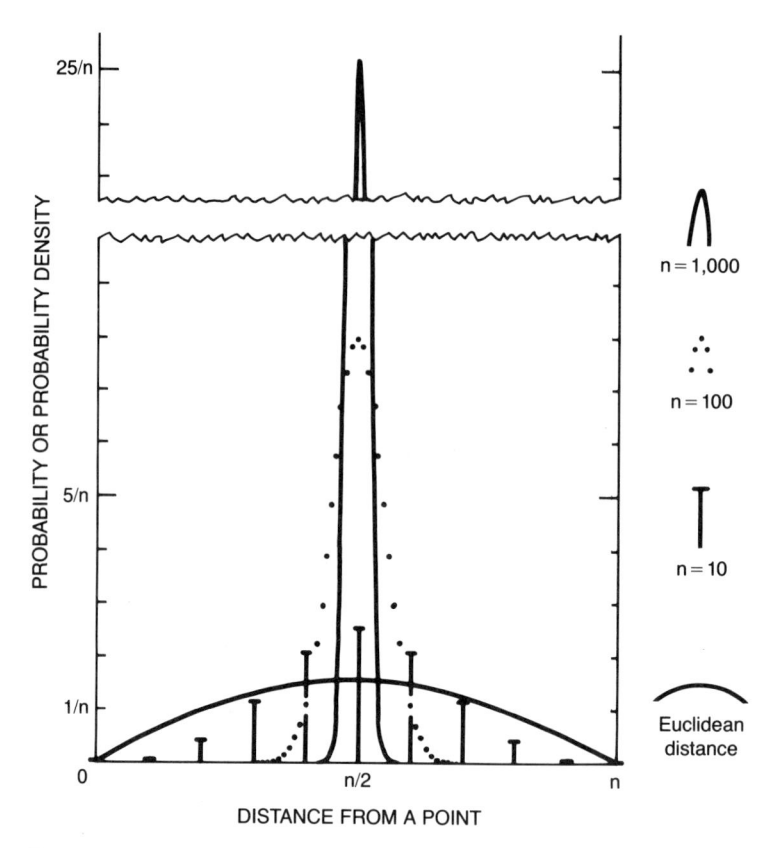

Figure 1.1
Distribution of Hamming distance in $\{0, 1\}^n$ and of Euclidean distance on a three-dimensional sphere with circumference $2n$.

and let the unknown length be c. Orient the triangle so that one point is the origin and the other two are A and B, with $|A| = a$ and $|B| = b$. Then the length c of the third side is $c = d(A, B) = |A - B|$.

From the triangle inequality (which applies because the space N with Hamming distance is a metric space) we know that the length of the third side is limited by the difference and the sum of the lengths of the other two ($|a - b| \leq c \leq a + b$), and naturally $c \leq n$. When A and B are sufficiently far from the origin and its complement (that is, $0 \ll a, b \ll n$), the distribution of c resembles the binomial distribution with parameters n and p, where

$$p = \frac{a}{n} + \frac{b}{n} - 2\frac{a}{n}\frac{b}{n}.$$

The mean value for the third side is then

$$E\{c\} = np = a + b - 2ab/n$$

and the variance is

$$\text{Var}\{c\} \cong npq, \quad q = 1 - p.$$

The mean and the variance of the third side, c, are derived in appendix A.

If the two known sides are equal, $a = b$, the probability p becomes $2(a/n)(1 - a/n)$, giving $2a(1 - a/n)$ as the mean length of the third side. We will use this result shortly. For now, notice that if two points A and B are taken at random near a third point, C, then C is nearly between A and B because $d(A, B) \cong d(A, C) + d(C, B)$. When the two points are at a distance $n/4$ from a third point ($a = b = n/4$), they are $1.5(n/4)$ from each other, on the average, which is at $\frac{3}{4}$ of the maximum distance that they could be.

Distribution of the Circle $O(r, x)$ Central to the memory model is that a region of addresses around an address is active at once. We shall therefore examine how the space N is distributed around a point. We shall answer two questions: (1) What is the area of (i.e., the number of points in) the circle $O(r, x)$? (2) How are the points of the circle distributed?

The area of the circle $O(r, x)$ is the number of points that are $0, 1, 2, \ldots, r$ bits from x; therefore, it is the sum of the first $r + 1$ binomial coefficients,

$$|O(r, x)| = \binom{n}{0} + \binom{n}{1} + \cdots + \binom{n}{r},$$

which, according to an earlier definition of $N(d)$, equals $N \cdot N(r)$. Its normal approximation is $N \cdot F\{(r - n/2)/\sqrt{n/4}\}$, where F is the normal distribution function. I will henceforth use r_p to denote the radius of a circle that

Table 1.2
Radii r_p of x-centered circles of N that enclose specified portions of the space N.

Portion p of the space N within r_p bits of point x	Number of dimensions, n					
	$n = 100$		$n = 1{,}000$		$n = 10{,}000$	
	r_p Bits	% of n	r_p Bits	% of n	r_p Bits	% of n
0.000000001	20	20	405	41	4,700	47.0
0.00000001	22	22	411	41	4,720	47.2
0.0000001	24	24	418	42	4,740	47.4
0.000001	26	26	425	42	4,760	47.6
0.00001	29	29	433	43	4,790	47.9
0.0001	31	31	441	44	4,810	48.1
0.0005	34	34	448	45	4,840	48.4
0.001	35	35	451	45	4,850	48.5
0.01	38	38	463	46	4,880	48.8
0.1	44	44	480	48	4,940	49.4
0.25	47	47	489	49	4,970	49.7
0.5	50	50	500	50	5,000	50

encloses p of N, and so, by definition, $N(r_p) = p$ and $|O(r_p, x)| = pN$. Notice that $r_{0.5} = n/2$. Table 1.2 shows selected values of r_p. (Tables 1.1 and 1.2 are different views of the same data.) What stands out again is that we need to take a large radius, close to $n/2$, to include much of N at all, and then, as r grows beyond $n/2$, almost all of the space is included at once.

Most of a circle that includes at most half of the space ($r \leq n/2$) lies very close to the periphery of the circle, as the following argument shows: Point x of N has n neighbors that are one bit away from it, $n(n-1)/2$ that are two bits away, $n(n-1)(n-2)/3!$ that are three bits away, and, in general, $(n:r)$ that are r bits away. For values of r that are small compared with n, the number grows nearly exponentially with r. (The neighborhood of a point on a sphere in Euclidean 3-space never grows faster than the square of r.) The ratio of two consecutive binomial coefficients $(n:r+1)$ and $(n:r)$ equals $(n-r)/(r+1)$, so that when $r < n/3$ a one-bit increase in r at least doubles the size of the circle. Over half of the points of such a circle are maximally far (r bits away) from the center. Incidentally, with $n = 1{,}000$, a radius of $n/3$, or 333 bits, inscribes only about 10^{-25} of the space.

The distribution of a circle that inscribes less than half of the space ($r < n/2$) is approximately binomial with parameters n and p, where p is slightly less than $2(r/n)(1 - r/n)$. Why? Because, first, most of a circle lies near its periphery, or at about r bits from the center, and, second, the distribution of the third side of a triangle with two known sides equal to r approximates the binomial distribution with the parameters given above. It is interesting and significant that when the radius is sufficiently close to the indifference distance $n/2$ (for example, $n/3 < r < n/2$), most of the points of a circle are nearly orthogonal to one another. This proves to be important in reading from memory by pooling data from a region of memory, as will become clear later.

Intersection of Two Circles Finally, we need to know by how much two circles of N overlap, as a function of their radii (the two radii are assumed to be equal) and the distance between their centers. That will allow us to study aspects of retrieval from the memory such as how close to a stored item a retrieval cue must be to effect the retrieval of the stored item.

The area of the intersection, derived in appendix B, is given by

$$I(d) = |O(r_p, x) \cap O(r_p, y)|$$
$$\cong N \int_{d/n}^{1} g(p, u) \, du,$$

where $d = d(x, y)$—the distance between the centers of the circles—and

$$g(p, u) = \frac{1}{2\pi\sqrt{u(1-u)}} \exp\left(-\frac{1}{2}\frac{c_p^2}{1-u}\right), \quad 0 < u < 1.$$

In the latter expression, c_p is the normalized distance from the edge of the circle to the equator and is therefore given by

$$c_p = N^{-1}(p) = (r_p - n/2)/\sqrt{n/4}.$$

The approximation is excellent when n is large and $0 \ll r_p \ll n$, as they are here, and then the intersection function is determined almost exclusively by p, which is the proportion of the space inscribed by r_p. Table 1.3 and figure 1.2 give the area of the intersection relative to the size of the circle for selected values of p.

Memory Items as Points of the Space $\{0, 1\}^n$

In this study, memory items are represented by n-component patterns of zeros and ones, with no particular meaning assigned to the components (they are abstract features). Bower (1967) used a similar representation in a formal study of the memory trace. In his study, points of the space A^n represent memory items, where A is an unordered set of v elements, $A = \{a_1, a_2, \ldots, a_v\}$. The memory items of the present study are equivalent to those of Bower's study when $v = 2$.

Table 1.3
Intersection of two congruent circles relative to circle size, $i(p,x)/p$.

x (distance between the centers of the circles relative to n)	p (circle size relative to N)						
	0.5	0.1	0.01	0.001	0.0001	0.00001	0.000001
0.000	1.000	1.000	1.000	1.000	1.000	1.000	1.000
0.001	0.980	0.956	0.933	0.915	0.900	0.887	0.876
0.002	0.972	0.937	0.905	0.880	0.859	0.841	0.825
0.005	0.955	0.901	0.850	0.811	0.779	0.751	0.726
0.01	0.936	0.860	0.789	0.735	0.691	0.653	0.619
0.02	0.910	0.802	0.704	0.631	0.572	0.522	0.480
0.04	0.872	0.721	0.587	0.493	0.420	0.361	0.313
0.06	0.842	0.659	0.502	0.396	0.318	0.258	0.212
0.08	0.817	0.608	0.434	0.322	0.244	0.187	0.145
0.1	0.795	0.562	0.377	0.263	0.188	0.136	0.100
0.15	0.747	0.468	0.267	0.160	0.0978	0.0608	0.0382
0.2	0.705	0.390	0.188	0.0948	0.0491	0.0258	0.0137
0.25	0.667	0.324	0.129	0.0543	0.0233	0.0102	0.00448
0.3	0.631	0.267	0.0866	0.0294	0.0102	0.0036	0.00128
0.35	0.597	0.216	0.0556	0.0149	0.0041	0.0011	0.00031
0.4	0.564	0.172	0.0339	0.0069	0.0014	0.0003	0.00006
0.5	0.500	0.1000	0.01000	0.00100	0.00010	0.00001	0.000001
0.6	0.436	0.0484	0.00179	0.00006	0.00000	0.00000	0.000000
0.7	0.369	0.0164	0.00012	0.00000			
0.8	0.295	0.0024	0.00000				
0.9	0.205	0.0000					
1.000	0.000						

Mathematical Foundations 25

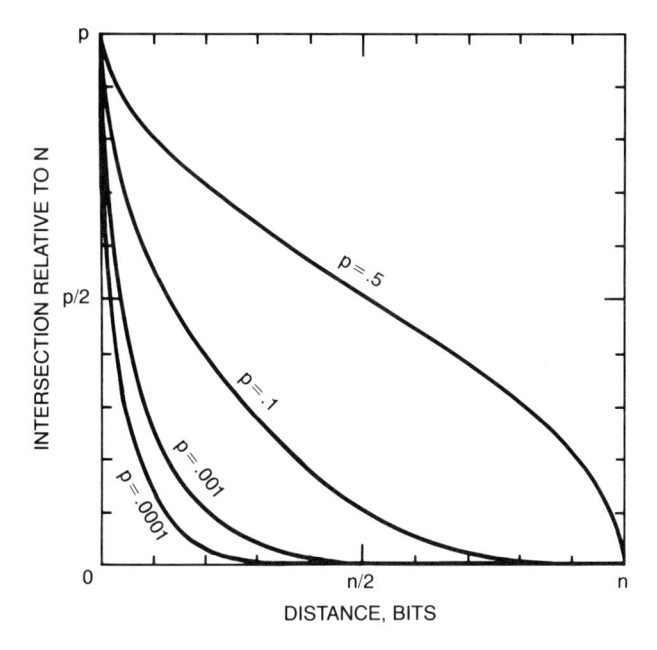

Figure 1.2
The intersection of two congruent circles, $i(x)$, as a function of the distance between their centers.

The distance between two points of $\{0, 1\}^n$ represents the similarity of two memory items—an association based on form. It is the number of places in which the two patterns differ, so that the closer the points, the more similar the items. Almost all of the space is nearly indifferent to (or about $n/2$ bits away from) any given point, whereas two points $n/4$ bits apart are very close to each other in the sense that an exceedingly small portion of the space lies within $n/4$ bits of a point. This is intuitively appealing in that any particular concept in our heads is unrelated to most other concepts, but any two unrelated concepts can be linked by a third that is closely related to both. In fact, there usually are many such "third" mediating concepts.

How are long binary words recognized as patterns? For an example, take a million random points of $\{0, 1\}^{1,000}$, representing a million memory items (prototype patterns) with 1,000 features each. A circle with a radius of 425 bits contains one millionth of the space. A memory item could then be thought of as the center of a circle with a radius somewhere around 425 bits. The patterns (points) inside the circle could be said to *belong to* the memory item, and the patterns outside it would possibly belong to some other item. Of course, there would be many borderline case—that is, possible patterns that have more than one nearest neighbor among the million memory items.

Now consider a recognition task in which a test item is presented to a subject, and assume that the item is one of the million items already in memory. How many features must be extracted to classify the test item—that is, so that the best match is to the right stored item? We just saw that a pattern should be closer than 425 bits from the stored item—say, within 400 bits (about 10^{-10} of the space lies within 400 bits of a point)—for the classification to be mostly correct. Therefore, it suffices to extract features with 0.6 probability of being correct.

Another way to look at it is that if 200 features (20 percent) can be determined with certainty, the remaining 800 features can be assigned zeros and ones at random, with probability 0.5, and the test item can still be recognized [because then the probability of a correct bit is $(0.2)(1) + (0.8)(0.5) = 0.6$]. This second interpretation could explain the recognition of an object in different contexts. If an object has 200 relevant features and the remaining 800 features represent the context or background, the object can be recognized once its 200 features have been identified correctly.

Although abstract and lacking in rigor, the ideas above should suggest the feasibility of long binary words as memory items. It was precisely the structure of the space $\{0, 1\}^n$, when n is large, that first made me interested in this approach to studying memory. The idea that the address space and the datum space should be the same occurred to me later, and later yet came the idea that the neuron was an ideal address decoder for such a memory.

Sets, Sequences or Lists, and Multisets

The standard primitive notion of a *set* is used. For example, $\{A, B, C\}$ is a set with three (distinct) elements, and $\{C, A, B\} = \{A, B, C\} = \{A, A, B, C\}$. In other words, the order of the elements and multiple occurrences of an element are ignored.

A *sequence* or a *list* is an ordered collection of objects (a k-tuple). The objects are called *elements*, and their number, including repeated occurrences of an element, is called the *length* of the sequence or list. For example, $\langle A, A, B, C \rangle$ is a sequence of length 4, and $\langle A, A, B, C \rangle \neq \langle A, B, C \rangle \neq \langle C, A, B \rangle$.

A *multiset* is an unordered collection of objects, much like a set except that any object may occur more than once. The objects are called *elements*, just as with sets. I will indicate a multiset by enclosing its elements in brackets. For example, $[A, A, B, C]$ is a multiset of size 4, and $[A, A, B, C] = [A, B, C, A] \neq [A, B, C]$.

Knuth (1981, p. 636) attributes the term multiset, if not the concept, to

N. G. de Bruijn. Patrick Suppes (personal communication) has suggested that a multiset be thought of as an equivalence class of lists under permutations. I would like to add that the multiset is a natural concept in probability and statistics. For example, a prototype for a problem in probability is drawing balls from a bag or an urn containing so many black balls and so many white balls. Here the bag or urn is a concrete example of a multiset. Speaking of the mean, or of some other statistic, of a multiset of values is clearly appropriate. Speaking of the mean of a *set* or values, however, is problematic, because the number of occurrences of any one value is lost.

A *multiunion* (denoted by ⊎) of two or more multisets is the multiset of the elements of the constituent multisets. For example,

$$[A, A, B] \uplus [A, B, C] = [A, A, A, B, B, C].$$

The number of elements of the multiunion is the sum of the number of elements of its constituent multisets,

$$|X \uplus Y| = |X| + |Y|,$$

which is the reason for the choice of the symbol ⊎.

Chapter 2
Background Material from Computers

Although the organization of memory in the brain need not resemble that in a computer, we should not dismiss outright the possibility that it does. At some level of abstraction, brains and computers can be treated as the same. But what is the lowest such level? The lower it is, the more useful computer concepts are in understanding memory in the brain. I feel that some correspondences are close enough to make a brief discussion of computer memories worthwhile.

Where should we look for the correspondences? The instruction set of any particular computer certainly seems irrelevant, and even the organization of programs into machine instructions and data may be irrelevant (some programming languages, most notably LISP, do not make this distinction). However, certain organizational features might be general enough to warrant our attention. In the following, I will focus on the division of a computer into two functional units, processor and memory, and on how computer memory is accessed.

With computer memories, we are in the fortunate position of knowing how they are constructed and what their function is. With the brain, we still mostly speculate, although we can say that information is stored in such a way that it will be retrieved by some cues and not by others, and even when retrieval fails we do not necessarily want to conclude that the information no longer is in memory. Rather, we should conclude that for the moment we do not have access to it. In computer terminology, we are addressing the memory with a wrong address.

The following facets of memory organization in a computer are relevant to the present discussion:

    the construction of memory from addressable locations,
    the distinction between address-decoder elements and storage elements,
    the fundamental role of address decoding in accessing the stored data (the address decoders map points of an abstract address space to physical storage locations), and
    the physical connection (wiring) of a storage location to an address decoder and to an outside source and destination of data.

The Random-Access Memory of a Computer

The memory of a computer is an array of *storage locations* or *registers*. A storage location stores information—typically, a binary word of a fixed length (i.e., the capacity of a location is finite).

A storage location is identified by its position in the memory array (a sequence number, called the *address* of the location). If a memory has N locations, they are referred to as locations $0, 1, 2, \ldots, N-1$, and the set $\{0, \ldots, N-1\}$ is called the *address space* of the memory.

The two operations of a computer memory are *writing* and *reading*, or *storage* and *retrieval*. To do either, it is necessary to specify an address first. The write operation then stores a word in the addressed location (the old contents of the location are replaced by the word being written), and the read operation retrieves a copy of the word stored last in the addressed location.

Several data paths are used to effect the transfer of data to and from memory: the memory address register (to hold the address of the location being accessed), the memory datum register (to hold the word being transferred to or from memory), and the lines for the read-command and write-command signals (to indicate the direction of the transfer). This organization is shown in figure 2.1. The processor exchanges data with the memory solely through the datum register.

The sequence of events in writing a word into memory is the following:

1. The processor loads the address register with the address in which the word is to be stored.
2. The processor loads the datum register with the word to be stored. (This step could precede step 1.)
3. The processor issues the write command.

In reading, the following steps are taken:

1. The processor loads the address register with the address of the location to be read.
2. The processor issues the read command.
3. The memory copies the contents of the addressed location into the datum register.

I will call a memory a *random-access* memory, as opposed to a *sequential-access* memory, if retrieval time is independent of the address of the storage location. The primary (core) memory of a computer is a random-access memory, but a magnetic tape clearly is not. A more precise characterization of a random-access memory, in terms of address decoding, is given below.

Address Decoding The address register provides input to the address decoders. The function of the address decoders is to find the addressed

Background Material from Computers   31

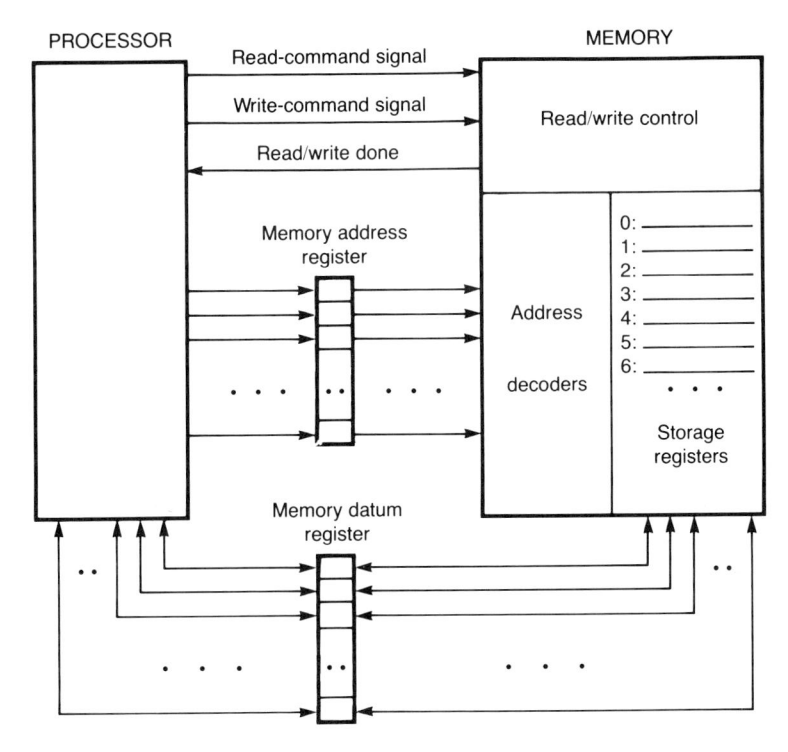

Figure 2.1
Data paths for accessing of memory by a computer. Arrows indicate direction of data flow.

location in the memory array and to activate it for the subsequent transfer of a word. The address decoders thus realize a selection function over the memory array.

An idealized address-decoder circuit has n input lines, one for each address bit, and N output lines ($N = 2^n$), one for each storage location. The n input lines can hold any combination of zeros and ones; however, in any given reference to memory, only one of the N output lines is 1 (for 'select'), and the rest are zeros.

The address-decoder circuit for a memory could be realized as N independent circuits, one for each storage location. Each one would have n inputs (the address lines) and one output (the select line), as shown in figure 2.2. A storage location i would then have its own private address decoder that realizes the selector or indicator function

$$A_i: N \to \{0, 1\}.$$

Now a more precise characterization of a random-access memory can be given: A memory is a random-access memory if the N selector functions

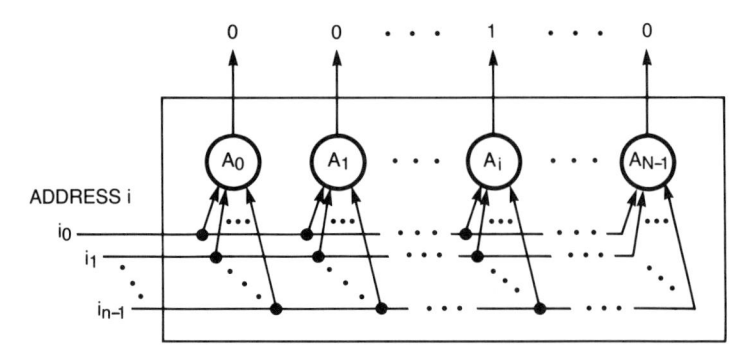

Figure 2.2
Address decoder $A: N \to \{0, 1\}^N$.

$A_i(x)$ are evaluated at once (in parallel) for all memory locations (for all i in N); it is a sequential-access memory if they are evaluated one at a time. That about half the circuits of a computer's memory perform address decoding tells something about the importance of address decoding to a random-access memory. The address decoders are truly a parallel computer.

Data Storage An h-bit storage location consists of h binary (bi-stable) storage elements, such as magnetic cores (small rings of magnetically active material) or simple semiconductor circuits (flip-flops). The organization of an h-bit storage location as h one-bit locations is shown in figure 2.3. In principle, a bit location is connected to the address decoder by a select line, to the datum register by a datum line, and to the processor by the read- and write-command-signal lines. The select signal and the write-command signal together cause writing into the location. Similarly, the select signal and the read-command signal together cause reading out of it.

Let us look at writing in detail. To write into a bit location requires that the input wires to the location be able to indicate one of three states: write 0, write 1, and no change (when the location is not selected for writing). If input wires have binary signals, at least two input wires are needed to represent the three states. In one possible realization of a bit location, one input wire would come from the address decoder and another would bring in the data bit being stored. I shall appeal to this architectural detail in chapter 9 when speculating about the loci of data storage in the brain.

Size of Memory A fairly large random-access memory of a modern computer has on the order of 2^{20} (a million) storage locations. The capacity of a location is typically in the range 32–64 bits, so we are speaking of memories with capacities of about 2^{26} bits. The address space of a 2^{20}-location memory naturally is $\{0, 1\}^{20}$.

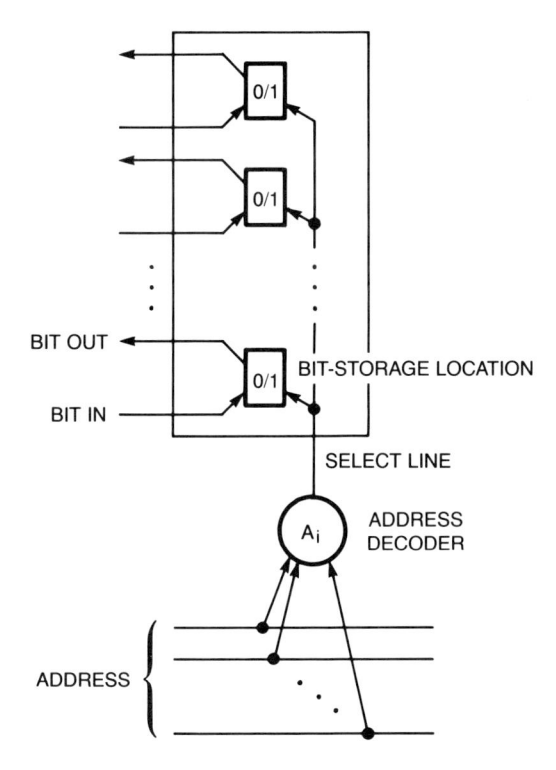

Figure 2.3
A storage location. Read- and write-command-signal lines are not shown.

The memories that I find theoretically interesting as models of human memory have address spaces in the range of $\{0, 1\}^{100}-\{0, 1\}^{10,000}$. Only in this range does the distribution of the space (distances between points) match some of our intuitive notions about relations between concepts. But such memories might seem impractical, as even the lower end of the range, 2^{100}, is an enormously large number. The theory becomes practical only after we abandon the requirement that *every* address be represented physically by an address decoder and a storage register, as discussed under the topic of sparse memory.

Content-Addressable Memories

The memory just described could be called a *conventional* random-access memory. A less common type is *content-addressable* memory (Foster 1976; Thurber 1976). It, too, is an array of storage locations, and each location can contain a binary word. However, a storage locations is accessed according to its contents rather than according to its position in the array. Any part of the word contained in a location can be made to serve as the address (the retrieval cue). For each operation, the processor must specify what part (what coordinates) are used as the address. For example, the processor might request the reading of all the words in which the first k bits match a given k-bit key. The memory need not contain any such words or it may contain one or several. If there are several, the memory "gives" them to the processor one at a time.

Each location of a content-addressable memory contains the circuits needed to determine whether there is a match. The circuits are effectively an address decoder, and a content-addressable memory can be made into an ordinary random-access memory by assigning permanently a part of each word (the first k bits, for example) to the address and the rest to the datum and by making sure in writing into memory that no two words are identical in their first k bits. The reason for having conventional random-access memories at all is that they are much cheaper to build than content-addressable memories.

An outstanding feature of conventional random-access memories is that a *unique* location is selected by each address; that is, given an address, exactly one location participates in the transfer of a word. In a content-addressable memory the selection need not be unique. However, it is based on an exact match in a designated subset of coordinates, or what could be called "identity of a part." In my memory model many locations are selected by a single address, but the criterion of selection is that the location's *address* be similar to the retrieval cue rather than that a part of the location's *contents* match the retrieval cue. The power of the model can be attributed to this mode of accessing the memory.

A warning about terminology: Computer professionals use the term *associative memory* to mean content-addressable memory as described above. In the literature of psychology, *content addressable* and *associative* are not necessarily synonymous. My memory model might be considered associative in the sense of the psychologist; however, it is definitely not content-addressable in the sense of the computer engineer, as the contents of a location have nothing to do with the location's being selected for a read or a write operation.

Chapter 3
Background Material from Idealized Neurons

The Neuron

A rather simplified description of a neuron is as follows: A neuron has a cell body with two kinds of branches: *dendrites* and an *axon* (figure 3.1). It receives input signals from other neurons, integrates (i.e., sums) them, and is capable of generating its own signal (an electric impulse that travels along the axon away from the cell body). The axon, in turn, makes contact with the dendrites and cell bodies of other neurons; thus, the output signal of one neuron becomes input to other neurons. The points of electric contact between neurons are called *synapses*.

When a neuron generates a signal, we say that it *fires*. After firing, the neuron must *recover* before it can fire again. Once it has recovered, its subsequent firing depends on the input that it receives.

The relative importance of a synapse to the firing of a neuron is called the *input coefficient* or synaptic *weight*. There are two kinds of synapses: *excitatory* synapses, which help a neuron to fire, and *inhibitory* synapses, which hinder firing. An entire mammalian neuron is either excitatory or inhibitory according to the kinds of synapses that its axon makes (Eccles 1975). In formal treatments of neurons, the weights of excitatory synapses are regarded as positive and those of inhibitory synapses as negative. Whether a recovered neuron actually fires depends on whether it has received sufficient excitatory input and not too much inhibitory input within the *period of latent addition*. In other words, only the most recent input affects the firing of a neuron.

In addition to input, the firing of a neuron depends on the neuron's *threshold*. The higher the threshold, the more important it is that the excitatory synapses have input and the inhibitory ones do not. If the threshold is sufficiently low, the neuron fires spontaneously once it has recovered from the previous firing.

Formal Neurons

The formal model of a neuron used here is attributed to McCulloch and Pitts (1943). In formal treatment of neural nets it is common to make further

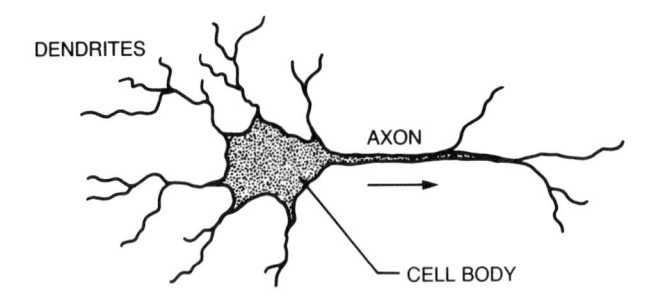

Figure 3.1
A neuron.

simplifying assumptions. The net is assumed to operate in synchronous time steps. Time is divided into intervals that stand for the period of latent addition. Within each such interval a neuron can fire at most once, and the firing during interval t depends solely on the neuron's inputs during interval $t-1$ and the threshold. The output is said to be 1 when the neuron fires and 0 otherwise.

An n-input neuron is then modeled by a *linear threshold function*

$$F: \{0,1\}^n \to \{0,1\}$$

as follows: For $i = 0, \ldots, n-1$, let F_t be the output at time t,

$$F_t \in \{0,1\};$$

let $x_{i,t}$ be the ith input at time t,

$$x_{i,t} \in \{0,1\};$$

let w_i be the weight of the ith input; and let c be the threshold. The *weighted sum* of the inputs is defined by

$$S_t = \sum_{i=0}^{n-1} w_i x_{i,t}.$$

The output is then given by

$$F_t = \begin{cases} 1 & \text{if } S_{t-1} \geq c \\ 0 & \text{otherwise,} \end{cases}$$

where $F_t = 1$ means that the neuron fires at time t and $F_t = 0$ that it does not. (See figure 3.2.) In other words, for a neuron to fire, the weighted sum must reach or exceed the threshold. Excitatory inputs increase the sum; inhibitory inputs decrease it. To maximize the sum, all excitatory inputs must be ones (on) and all inhibitory inputs must be zeros (off).

It should be noted in passing that a linear threshold function with binary

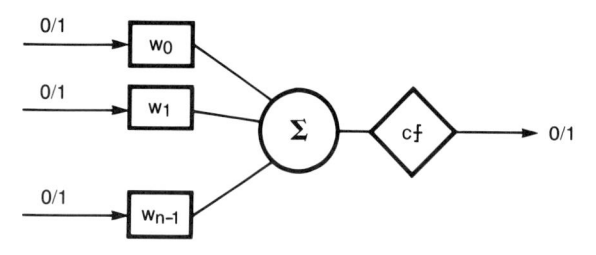

Figure 3.2
A linear threshold function.

arguments (each input is either 0 or 1) is a Boolean function. However, most Boolean functions of n variables cannot be expressed as linear threshold functions over $\{0, 1\}^n$.

The simplifying assumptions about the neuron could be criticized on several grounds. The central nervous system does not operate synchronously. The period of latent addition and the length of recovery vary from neuron to neuron, and they need not stay constant over time even for an individual neuron. The following could be a better description of recovery after firing: Firing raises the neuron's threshold to a value greater than the maximum weighted sum, and the neuron cannot fire again immediately. Thereafter, the threshold drops until firing becomes possible. It could continue to drop indefinitely, even until the neuron fires spontaneously. However, even if this were closer to what actually happens, it would not affect the conclusions of this study.

The linear-threshold model of a neuron is itself an idealization. For my results, it is sufficient that the neuron function be a threshold function (it does not have to be linear) and that some neurons have both excitatory and inhibitory inputs.

Finally, I want to draw attention to one way in which stimulus *intensity* is encoded in the nervous system: It is often translated into firing *frequency*, which in turn can be viewed as the *probability* that a certain bit of a datum is 1 at a given time. Thus, at least in some instances, the nervous system apparently digitizes information to facilitate computation and the transmission of data (and maybe even data storage—less is known about that). Not surprisingly, an engineer converts analog signals to digital to improve control over computation and over the transmission of data.

Modeling with Neurons: The Perceptron

Think of the n inputs to a formal neuron as an n-component pattern of zeros and ones. Clearly, then, a neuron divides all possible input patterns into two sets: the patterns that cause it to fire and those that do not. The sets are said to be *linearly separable*, because their separation is affected by a linear threshold function. Hence, a linearly separable set A is defined by $n + 1$ real numbers or parameters—the n input coefficients w_i and the threshold c—according to the formula

$$x \in A \text{ iff } \sum_{i=0}^{n-1} w_i x_i \geq c$$

(i.e., the weighted sum is at least c for all elements of A and it is less than c for all elements of the complement of A). The inequality defines a hyperplane that cuts through the n-dimensional pattern space. Thus, a neuron seems to be an appropriate device for pattern classification.

A more interesting aspect of a neuron is its potential for learning, in a finite number of trials, any linearly separable set, irrespective of the initial values of the neuron's parameters. This result is known as the *perceptron-convergence theorem*. That such learning by real neurons actually takes place is but a hypothesis.

The linear-threshold neuron with modifiable synapses is an essential component of a neural-circuit model called the *perceptron*. Rosenblatt (1958, 1962) introduced it for the study of computation by neural nets. Later, Minsky and Papert (1969) studied the perceptron's ability to compute geometric predicates (for which they coined the term *computational geometry*).

A simple perceptron is a two-layer network. The first layer is a set of neurons with inputs from a "retina" that holds a (geometric) pattern. The second layer is a (linear-threshold) neuron that receives its inputs from the first layer. Its output is the output of the perceptron. (See figure 3.3.) The

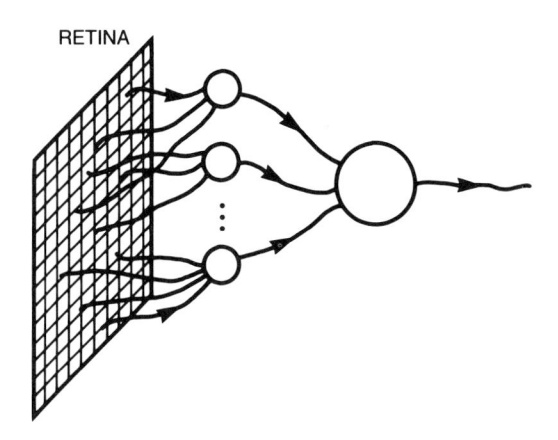

Figure 3.3
A two-layer perceptron.

question then is: What kinds of patterns can a perceptron recognize if the complexity of the first-layer neurons is restricted in certain ways? Another question of interest, of course, concerns the ability of a perceptron to learn to recognize *any* linearly separable set; here the perceptron-convergence theorem states the positive result. In addition to the simple two-layer perceptron, Rosenblatt studied perceptrons with more layers and with feedback. Nilsson (1965) discusses learning models based on these ideas.

A Critical Look at Perceptron-Convergence Learning

It is commonly believed that changes in synaptic connections—that is, in the neurons' input coefficients—account for learning. That view is theoretically backed by the perceptron-convergence theorem. I want to examine the idea critically and, in particular, to try to see how to realize learning by adjusting the input coefficients of neurons.

Learning by the adjusting of input coefficients would take place in roughly the following manner: Assume that a neuron is to learn to differentiate between two sets, A and B, of input patterns, and assume that the task is possible (i.e., that the two sets are linearly separable from one another). The training involves presenting a random sequence of elements of A and B together with the information as to whether an element is from A or B—that is, sampling and reinforcement. The neuron learns by adjusting its parameters after every failure to classify an element. In any trial, the new weights and the new threshold are functions of the sample element and the present weights and threshold. The present values of the parameters are the only memory about the past. The perceptron-convergence theorem shows that, regardless of the initial weights and threshold, the neuron can learn to distinguish elements of A from elements of B in a finite number of trials.

In the next chapter I will show that the signs of the input coefficients define a binary address (a point of $\{0, 1\}^n$) and that the threshold defines the size of a region to which the neuron responds. In those terms, perceptron convergence means finding an address and a surrounding region that includes set A and excludes set B.

The description of perceptron convergence and the contexts in which the topic appears in the literature (e.g., the computing of geometric predicates) suggest that patterns are presented as input to a neuron and that a neuron is trained to recognize a set of patterns. But this cannot be done without additional mechanisms. So let us look into the underlying assumptions of learning by perceptron convergence. What troubles me is that learning of this kind seems to require quite powerful support mechanisms. They might have to be powerful enough to perform, by themselves, any discrimination that could be taught to a neuron.

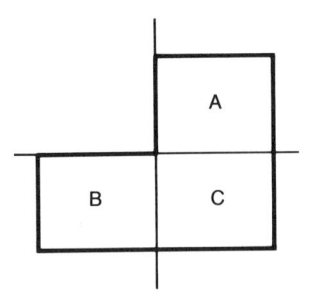

Figure 3.4
Two pairs of linearly separable sets.

The fundamental problem lies in identifying a neuron or a set of neurons that is to learn a particular distinction. The perceptron-convergence theorem shows that the convergence to proper weights is independent of the initial weights—that is, that any neuron can be trained to make any distinction that is possible for a neuron. In other words, the initial parameters of the neuron do not matter. Thus, for different neurons to learn different things, either the sampling of input or the reinforcement must be directed, and the directing must be more or less permanent. I will demonstrate this with an example.

Consider the learning of more than one distinction. Let A, B, and C be three nonempty sets of patterns, and let A be linearly separable from $B \cup C$ and B be linearly separable from $A \cup C$. (See figure 3.4.) Assume that the organism must learn to discriminate between the sets A and $B \cup C$ and, at the same time, between the sets B and $A \cup C$. The following argument shows that at least two neurons (hyperplanes) are needed for these two tasks.

Assume that a neuron has been trained to separate A from $B \cup C$. Then the same neuron cannot separate B from $A \cup C$, because it would have to separate B from C. Another neuron must therefore be trained to separate B from $A \cup C$. Call these two neurons the A-neuron and the B-neuron, respectively. Assume that the two neurons are identical at the start, that an element of A is presented, and that both neurons respond with 1. Then the A-neuron is right and should be left alone, but the B-neuron is wrong and should be adjusted. In other words, the organism (or the environment) must administer reinforcement selectively, and for the training to be successful, the selection must, by and large, remain the same from trial to trial.

The implicit assumptions of learning distinctions by adjusting input weights thus seem to be the following: The organism—and not the neuron—must assign neurons to discriminations (to pairs of linearly separable subsets of the pattern space), it must recognize which particular discrimination a sample item and the accompanying reinforcement refer to, and it must select the right neuron or neurons for reinforcement. This requires the addressing of neurons by pairs of subsets of the pattern space (this neuron is assigned to—it will be taught to discriminate between—the $\{A, B \cup C\}$ pair, and that neuron is assigned to the $\{B, A \cup C\}$ pair). But having such addressing implies that the discrimination problem has already been solved! The fixed addressing that is needed to direct reinforcement to the proper neurons represents computation that is at least as complex as the discrimination that a (linear-threshold) neuron is capable of learning. This is the essence of what I call the selection problem (or accessing problem, or addressing problem) in learning to recognize patterns by adjusting input coefficients.

This criticism points to an important conclusion: Even if some neurons have adjustable synapses and if such synapses store information, there is also the need for a fixed accessing mechanism that *selects* the synapses in which the information is stored and from which it is retrieved under any given set of circumstances. The accessing mechanism would be a *permanent frame of reference*, and it would correspond to the address-decoder circuits of a computer memory. Furthermore, it seems that *an encoding of the present situation or circumstance should serve as the address.*

Chapter 4
Neurons as Address Decoders

My thesis is that certain classes of neurons should have their input coefficients (and their thresholds) fixed over the entire life of an organism. For reasons that will soon be made clear, I shall call such neurons *address-decoder neurons*. According to this interpretation, the n-tuple of input coefficients determines an n-bit address—a pattern to which the neuron responds most readily—and the threshold controls the size of the region of similar address patterns to which the neuron responds. This interpretation of the neuron function as an address decoder is the first major insight of this study.

In the remainder of this chapter, the input coefficients of a neuron are assumed to be constant in time, whereas the threshold is allowed to vary. Different neurons, by and large, and assumed to have different input coefficients.

Let us look first at a simple linear threshold function $U(x)$ of four variables, with weights 1, -1, -1, and -1 and threshold 0:

$$U(x) = 1 \text{ iff } u(x) \geq 0,$$

where $u(x) = x_0 - x_1 - x_2 - x_3$. Table 4.1 shows the entire function. The fourth column gives the distances between the points of the space and 1000. Notice that the function $U(x)$ is 1 whenever this distance is no more than 1. If the threshold were increased from 0 to 1, the function $U(x)$ would be 1 only when $x = 1000$.

Input Coefficients and the Address of a Neuron

The *address*, a, of a neuron with input coefficients w, where $w = \langle w_0, \ldots, w_{n-1} \rangle$, is defined as the n-bit input pattern that maximizes the weighted sum. The maximum occurs when the inhibitory inputs are zeros and the excitatory inputs are ones, and so the ith bit of the address is

$$a_i = \begin{cases} 1 & \text{if } w_i > 0 \\ 0 & \text{if } w_i < 0 \end{cases}$$

(we assume for now that all weights are nonzero). The *maximum weighted sum*, $S(w)$, is then the sum of the positive coefficients:

Table 4.1
The linear function $u(x) = x_0 - x_1 - x_2 - x_3$ and the threshold function $U(x)$ with threshold 0.

x	$u(x)$	$U(x)$	$d(1000, x)$
0000	0	1	1
0001	−1	0	2
0010	−1	0	2
0011	−2	0	3
0100	−1	0	2
0101	−2	0	3
0110	−2	0	3
0111	−3	0	4
1000	1	1	0
1001	0	1	1
1010	0	1	1
1011	−1	0	2
1100	0	1	1
1101	−1	0	2
1110	−1	0	2
1111	−2	0	3

$$S(w) = \sum_{w_i > 0} w_i.$$

The point opposite the neuron's address, 'a, yields the *minimum weighted sum*, $s(w)$, which is the sum of the negative coefficients:

$$s(w) = \sum_{w_i < 0} w_i.$$

For brevity, we let S stand for the maximum sum $S(w)$ and let s stand for the minimum sum $s(w)$. (See figure 4.1.) In the example at the beginning of the chapter (and in table 4.1), the input coefficients are 1, −1, −1, and −1, the maximum weighted sum is 1 and the pattern corresponding to it (the neuron's address) is 1000, and the minimum weighted sum is −3 and the pattern corresponding to it is 0111.

The Threshold and the Response Region of a Neuron

When the threshold c is in the range $s < c \leq S$, the output of the neuron is 0 for some addresses (input patterns) and 1 for others. If the threshold is above S, the output is always 0; if it is below s, the output is always 1.

By a proper choice of the threshold, a neuron responds to just one address; that is, when the threshold is S (the maximum for the weighted

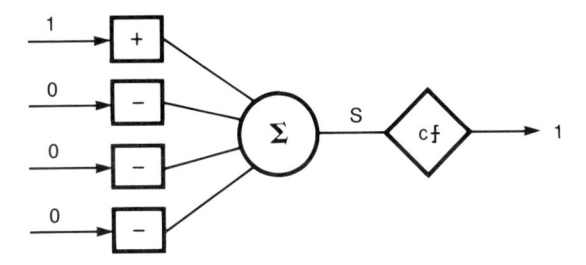

Figure 4.1
The address of a neuron.

sum), the neuron responds only to its own address and acts like an address decoder of a conventional computer memory.

What, exactly, happens when the threshold decreases from S to s? First, consider the simple case where all positive weights have value 1, all negative weights have value -1, and no weight is 0. Let a be the address of a neuron, let P be the number of positive weights, let Q be the number of negative weights ($P + Q = n$), let d be a distance ($d \geq 0$), and let $c = S - d$ be the threshold. Then $S = P$ and $s = -Q$. Let the threshold c decrease from S to s. This corresponds to letting the distance d increase from 0 to n. Then, for any given d, the neuron responds to all the addresses that are within d bits of the neuron's address a. These addresses form a region around a, called the *response region* of the neuron, with point a at the center of the region. The exact size of the region (the number of points) as a function of distance d is the size of the circle $O(d, a)$ and is equal to $N \cdot N(d)$, where $N(d)$ is the distribution function for the space $\{0, 1\}^n$ (see the subsections on "Distribution of the Space N" and "Distribution of a Circle" in chapter 1). Thus, for small values of d the response region grows slowly with d, but in the neighborhood of $d = n/2$ the region grows very rapidly to include most of the address space.

If the firing of a neuron is taken to mean that a pattern has been recognized, a neuron is best thought of as a pattern-recognition device for a single pattern (point) rather than for some linearly separable set of patterns. This pattern is the neuron's address, and it is common to all nonempty, linearly separable sets that are obtained from a given set of input coefficients by varying the threshold. If the neuron's address a is thought of as a prototype or target pattern and an address x is thought of as a sample pattern, the neuron "recognizes" x if x is sufficiently close to (or within the distance $S - c$ of) the neuron's address. The comparison is indifferent to the location of the mismatched bits; only their number matters.

Here the threshold, c, serves as a gauge. To accept (or recognize) only closely matching patterns—that is, patterns that differ from the target pattern by only a small number of bits—c must be almost as high as the maximum weighted sum, S. When the threshold is lowered, more and more patterns are recognized. In the example at the beginning of this chapter, threshold 1 would make the function 1 only for the pattern 1000, threshold 0 makes it 1 for all patterns within one bit of 1000, threshold -1 would make it 1 for all patterns within two bits of 1000, and threshold -2 would make it 1 for all patterns but 0111. A neuron thus seems suited for pattern classification by the *nearest-neighbor method*, which assigns a test pattern to the stored pattern that is most similar to the test pattern. This property of neurons will be used in constructing a best-match machine in the next chapter.

Unequal Weights and Weighted Distance

This section is included for completeness. Its purpose is to show that unequal input weights do not affect the nature of the theory. The remainder of this study is then carried out with the simplifying assumption that all input weights are 1s and -1s.

Assume that the input weights can have values other than 1 and -1. The response region is still centered around the neuron's address, but in general there is no single distance d that would describe the border of the region. However, if some point x is in the response region of a neuron, so are all the points between x and the neuron's address. With unequal input weights, the absolute value of a coefficient is a measure of an input's relative importance to the firing of a neuron.

A slightly more general notion of distance is useful in dealing with unequal weights. Define the *weighted distance* between points x and y as

$$\sum_{i=0}^{n-1} |w_i||y_i - x_i|.$$

Notice that $|y_i - x_i|$ is 0 or 1 according to whether the ith coordinates of x and y agree or differ (it is the exclusive-or function). The weighted distance can also be thought of as a *generalized Hamming distance*,

$$\sum_{i=0}^{n-1} |y'_i - x'_i|,$$

in the n-dimensional space obtained by mapping the zeros and ones of an address z to zeros and $|w_i|$'s of z' as follows:

$$z'_i = |w_i|z_i.$$

Geometrically, instead of the points of the space being at the vertices of an n-dimensional cube with sides of length 1, they are the vertices of an n-dimensional (rectangular) parallelepiped with sides of length $|w_i|$, and the

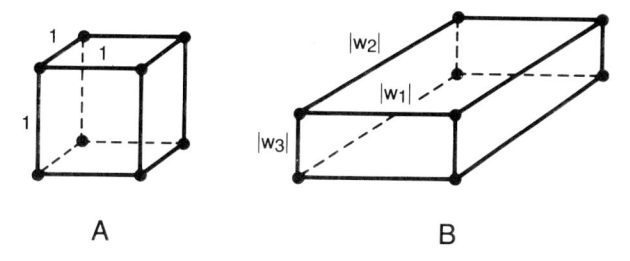

Figure 4.2
Equal (A) and unequal (B) input weights.

generalized Hamming distance between two points is the length of the shortest path between them along the edges of the parallelepiped. (See figure 4.2.)

Multiplying the weights and the threshold by a positive constant does not affect the behavior of a neuron. Therefore, we will assume that the weights are normalized to make their absolute values add to n,

$$\sum_{i=0}^{n-1} |w_i| = n,$$

which makes $S - s = n$. When the absolute weights are equal and nonzero, the weighted distance is the Hamming distance.

The size of the response region (the number of points), as a function of the weighted distance, is approximately normal, with mean $n/2$ and variance

$$\tfrac{1}{4} \sum_{i=0}^{n-1} w_i^2.$$

(The normal approximation of the binomial distribution, which we get when the absolute weights are equal, is a special case of this. In both cases we have the sum of n independent random variables.) Thus, as the threshold decreases from S to s, the response region grows in much the same way as it does in the case of equal absolute weights. The unevenness of weights simply makes the distribution flatter and the growth of the region about the (mean) distance $(S - s)/2$ ($= n/2$) less sudden.

We will now relax the condition that all weights be nonzero. An input with a zero coefficient means simply that the neuron is indifferent to the value of that input; it could just as well be removed. When some of the coefficients are zeros, the neuron's address is no longer uniquely defined in the n-dimensional address space. However, the response region for all values of the threshold is well defined, and the region corresponding to the maximum weighted sum S could be used as the address of the neuron. It is a subspace of the original space.

The address-decoder function of a neuron is robust. The strength of a synapse is relatively unimportant, for a neuron's address is affected by two things only: the adding or removing of inputs and the change of sign of an input coefficient. The first is manifested in the growth of new synapses and the deletion of old ones. If such changes are not numerous in comparison with the total number of (input) synapses of a neuron, the neuron's address will not be affected greatly. The second would change the neuron's address more drastically; however, as far as is known, synapses do not change from excitatory to inhibitory or vice versa, as the outputs of any one neuron are either all excitatory or all inhibitory. A change of sign is possible but would require the insertion of an intermediate neuron of the opposite kind between the two neurons that form the original synapse. All in all, it does not seem likely that an input coefficient would change sign. This would be a further constraint on perceptron-convergence learning.

In adopting the linear-threshold model, we have ignored the possible effects of the geometry of the dendrites and the positions of the synapses on them and on the cell body. Even if such effects were pronounced, the neuron would still act as an address decoder according to our definition. Only the shape of the response region would be affected.

Chapter 5
Search of Memory for the Best Match

The Problem of the Best Match

This chapter is a bridge from the neuron model to the memory model. As the first application of the unifying principle, which states that the data stored in memory are addresses to the memory, I will describe a computer —the *Best-Match Machine*—that is well suited for solving a problem that is hard for a conventional computer. The construction of the Best-Match Machine gives an idea of what the final memory model of this study is like.

Consider the problem of finding the best match to a test word in a data set of stored words. Minsky and Papert discuss this in their book *Perceptrons* (1969) under the heading "Time vs. Memory for Best Matching: An Open Problem" (pp. 222–225). The problem is the following: Describe a filing scheme for storing a set X of words (a data set of n-bit binary numbers; I have changed their nomenclature to conform with mine) so that one can retrieve, in minimum time, the stored word ζ that is the best match to a test word z. (The Greek letters ξ, η, and ζ will be used for words of the data set, with the target word denoted by ζ.) "Best match" means closest to in Hamming distance. The data set is assumed to fall randomly on the 2^n possible words (the data set has no particular structure), and the test words, likewise, are a random sample of the 2^n words. The question is: How does retrieval time depend on memory size?

Minsky and Papert conclude on a rather pessimistic note. They find an encouraging solution only when memory size is at least $2^n n$ bits—that is, when there is an n-bit storage location for every possible n-bit word. Filing the data X consists of storing at each address the word of X that matches the address the best. Retrieval is then reduced to reading just one word, or n bits, from the location addressed by the test word.

The effort that goes into filing the data set is not dealt with in *Perceptrons*. The filing for the above scheme requires the accessing of all of memory, and much of it more than once. The following might be a reasonable filing scheme: First store the words of the data set at locations addressed by the words themselves. Then, for each word ξ of the data set, compute all the words of N that are one bit away from ξ and write ξ in locations addressed by these distance-1 words, unless a location is already occupied (assume that each memory location has an extra location-occupied bit). Repeat this for distances 2, 3, and so on until all of memory is filled. Various criteria can be used to stop the checking of further locations around the word ξ. For example, if all addresses at distance d from ξ are found to be occupied (because they are closer to other words in the data set), further checking around ξ is unnecessary. In any case, with n but a modest 100, the memory will have 2^{100} (about 1,000,000,000,000,000,000,000,000,000,000) locations. So it would take less time to check each word of a trillion-word data set against each word of a trillion-word test set than to load the 2^{100}-location memory in the first place.

What I wanted to dramatize with this example is that conventional computer architecture does not seem to be suited for dealing with the problem of the best match. So let us examine how we might build a memory from neuronlike components to cope with the problem.

The Best-Match Machine

We have seen that a neuron can function as an address decoder for a storage location. A proper choice of the threshold makes a neuron respond to, or decode, just one address, and further lowering of the threshold makes it decode a set of addresses centered around that one address.

Consider a memory with N locations, where $N = 2^n$. Let each location have the capacity for one n-bit word (e.g., 2^{100} 100-bit words, just as in the example above), and let the address decoding be done by N address-decoder neurons of the kind discussed in chapter 4. (We will henceforth refer to an address-decoder neuron by its address x.) Set the threshold of each neuron x to its maximum weighted sum, $|x|$, and use a common parameter d to adjust all thresholds when accessing the memory. The effective threshold of neuron x will then be $|x| - d$, which means that the location x is accessible every time that the address x is within d bits of the address presented to the memory (i.e., the address held by the address register; see figure 2.1). With $d = 0$ we have a conventional random-access memory—the kind that, in the preceding section, proved unsuited to the problem of the best match. Assume, further, that each location has a special location-occupied bit that can be accessed in the same way as the regular datum bits. Writing a word to a location sets the location-occupied bit. Assume also that only occupied locations can be read.

To file the data, start by setting $d = n$ and issue a command to clear the location-occupied bit. This single operation marks all of memory as unoccupied, regardless of the value of the address register. Then set $d = 0$ and write each word ξ of the data set with ξ itself as the address. Notice that each write operation affects only one location: the location ξ. Filing time is thus proportional to the number of words in the data set.

Finding the best match for a test word, z, involves placing z in the address register and finding the least distance d for which there is an occupied location. We can start the search by setting $d = 0$ and incrementing d by one successively until an occupied location is found. This method gives average search times that are proportional to the number of address bits, or slightly less than $n/2$, because the nearest occupied location can be expected to be just under $n/2$ bits from z. A binary search on d would be even faster, terminating in $\log_2(n)$ steps.

The apparent need for an enormously large memory seems like a serious objection to this solution. With 100-bit words, 2^{100} locations would be needed. But *if we construct the memory as we store the words of the data set*, we need only one location (and one address decoder) for each word of the data set. None of the unoccupied locations need be present. This aspect of *sparseness*, in a different form, together with the storing of addresses as data, carries over to later memory models.

The reader may feel cheated by my solution, thinking that I made up the rules of the game as I went along, to suit my purposes. But that brings up the exact point I want to make: that the architecture of a computer determines what the computer is good for.

In addition to the problem of the *best* match, Minsky and Papert discuss time versus memory for an *exact* match. Their measure of time is the number of bits retrieved from memory, and the best solution, in a certain sense, is hash coding (a technique known to programmers). I have used the number of memory cycles as the measure, but neither it nor the number of bits retrieved really measures computation if we maintain that the accessing of memory is a form of computing, the amount of which depends on memory size. More is said about this in the next section.

The problem of the best match is a mathematician's problem. To solve it, even with the Best-Match Machine, requires that the machine be reliable (deterministic). If there is any slack, as there usually is in biological systems, the best match is no longer guaranteed. But a somewhat unreliable Best-Match Machine would still find a *good* match, and that is usually sufficient in emulating biological systems. The hash-coding solution for finding an exact match breaks down completely if the computer memory is unreliable. So here, again, the neuron memory shows its robustness in the kinds of tasks that it might be asked to perform.

The Best-Match Machine with Different Data To solve the problem of the best match, we stored the word ξ of the data set in location ξ. In the learning of sequences, we want to store some other word η in location ξ. If the Best-Match Machine is used in that way, what is retrieved by reading with the address x? We will only touch on this question here; we will return to it in chapter 8.

Let us assume that the data set contains word pairs $\langle \xi_i, \eta_i \rangle$, where the first word, ξ_i, is the address of the location in which the second word, η_i, is stored. Let us assume further that no two words are to be stored in the same location (i.e., $\xi_i \neq \xi_j$ for $i \neq j$; notice that the data in the best-match problem can be expressed as pairs $\langle \xi_i, \xi_i \rangle$). Reading from memory with address x will then find the occupied location that is closest to x (say, ξ_j), and will retrieve its contents, η_j (that is, the word that is stored at the address that matches x the best). If the pairs $\langle \xi_i, \eta_i \rangle$ themselves are thought of as a *partial* function $W: N \to N$, with $W(\xi_i) = \eta_i$, the Best-Match Machine extends the function into a *total* function by defining $W(x)$ as the value of the function at the nearest point where the partial function is defined.

A Note on Serial and Parallel Computing

The notions of serial and parallel computing have come up in the discussion. I want to clarify these notions and dispose of some common misconceptions.

We tend to think of the operation of a computer as serial because instructions are obeyed sequentially. However, many components of a computer are parallel processors. Parallelism is most striking in decoders such as instruction, device, and memory-address decoders, as has already been pointed out. Although by design the decoding usually results in a unique selection, we should appreciate the fact that this selection involves a great deal of parallel computation. The selection function is evaluated by every element that is capable of responding; however, by design the value of the function is 1 (for 'select') for just one element and 0 for all the others. Accordingly, *the mere accessing of memory should be regarded as computing*, the amount of which increases with memory size.

Computer programmers are familiar with the trade-off between run time and memory size. I suggest that the trade-off is really between serial and parallel computing. When the use of more memory actually allows us to write a faster program, we are, in fact, taking advantage of *parallel computing by the address decoders*. In contrast, a Turing machine is truly sequential, and with it we immediately notice the effect of memory size (i.e., the length of the active portion of the tape) on the amount of computing (number of steps, run time) required to access the memory. Similarly, increasing the size of the alphabet or the number of states of a Turing machine often allows us to write faster and more compact Turing-machine algorithms for a given task. But again, the use of a larger alphabet or a larger state space involves choosing from a greater number of alternatives. In any physical realization, that means more (parallel) computing in the form of decoding.

Chapter 6
Sparse Memory

We have seen thus far that a random-access memory is suited for pattern matching provided that linear threshold functions are used for address decoding, and that neurons can therefore serve as address decoders for such a memory. In this and the next chapter, we will see that the memory is practical and that the address-decoder neurons can be set in advance to their particular address patterns.

We will start with the foremost problem of the theory: the vastness of the address space N. There is no way to construct a random-access memory that has, say, $2^{1,000}$ storage locations. Even 2^{100} locations would be too many to fit into the human brain, as 2^{100} molecules of water would more than fill it (the number of neurons in the nervous system is "only" about 2^{36}). With such a vast address space, most of the addresses cannot be represented by an address decoder and a storage location. However, there is hardly the need for $2^{1,000}$ locations, because a human lifetime is too short to store anywhere near $2^{1,000}$ independent entities (a century has fewer than 2^{32} seconds).

A word could be stored in memory by writing it in a free storage location and at the same time providing the location with the appropriate address decoder. This possibility was mentioned in the discussion of the Best-Match Machine, and it is how a content-addressable computer memory works. However, the content-addressable memories of today's computers do not retrieve data on the basis of the similarity of the location's address to the retrieval cue, as is required by our model. (Recall that, in a content-addressable memory, an exact match with a designated part of a stored word causes the location to be selected; that part functions as the address of the location.) A neuron as an address decoder would select a location on the basis of similarity of address. However, it would then be necessary to set the neuron's address, once and for all, at the time of writing in the storage location, and that is a very difficult task to be accomplished with neurons. It would require first the identification of a free location (which in itself is an addressing problem) and then the setting of an address decoder for it (which would be complicated because synapses do not change from excitatory to inhibitory, or vice versa).

The alternative that I will explore here has the following characteristics:

The storage locations and their addresses are given from the start, and only the contents of the locations are modifiable.

The storage locations are very few in comparison with 2^n (the memory is sparse).

The storage locations are distributed randomly in the $\{0, 1\}^n$ address space.

I shall call such a memory a *sparse* random-access memory.

We have already seen that linear threshold functions are ideal for address decoding and that neurons act like linear threshold functions. But neurons are also suitable for storing data. We will see that the storage of data in a location could be realized by a set of counters. An address-decoder neuron with fixed input synapses and modifiable output synapses could function as a storage location.

Concepts Related to Sparse Memory

Multiset N' of Hard Locations   The storage locations N' of a sparse memory —more precisely, the addresses of the locations—are a uniform random sample, with replacement, of the address space N. They will be called simply *locations*. To emphasize that they are physical locations of a sparse memory, they will also be called *hard* locations. Logically, the hard locations N' are a multiset; however, since only very sparse memories are considered here—say, 2^{-980} (i.e., 2^{20} hard locations out of $2^{1,000}$ possible locations)—repetitions of an element can be ignored, and so the hard locations can be thought of as a set. The prime symbol (') on a lowercase letter will be used to indicate elements of N', so that x' refers to a hard address. The symbol N' will also be used for the number of (hard) locations of the sparse memory.

Distance to a Hard Location   Hard locations will be referred to by their addresses—for example, x'. By the *distance* from a point y (the address y) to a location x' is meant the distance $d(y, x')$ between the two addresses. Similarly, by the distance between two locations is meant the distance between their addresses.

Nearest N'-Neighbor, x'   The element of N' most similar to the element x of N is called the *nearest N'-neighbor* of x and is denoted by x' (x' is the hard location nearest to x). That x may have several nearest neighbors in N' is irrelevant to the discussion that follows. If X is a subset of N, then X' denotes the set of nearest N'-neighbors of elements of X:

$$X' = \{x' | x \in X\}.$$

Distance to the Nearest Location, $d(x, x')$ The distribution of distances from points of N to their nearest N'-neighbors can be derived from the distribution of N. The distances in N are distributed according to $N(d)$:

$$N(d) = \Pr\{d(x, y) \leq d | x, y \in N\}.$$

The distribution of $d(x, x')$, denoted here by $N'(d)$, where

$$N'(d) = \Pr\{d(x, x') \leq d\},$$

can then be obtained as follows: The probability that none of N' independent random points of N is within d bits of x is $[1 - N(d)]^{N'}$, so the probability that at least one is within d bits of X is given by

$$N'(d) = 1 - [1 - N(d)]^{N'}.$$

This can be rewritten as

$$N'(d) = 1 - [1 - N'N(d)/N']^{N'},$$

which is approximated by

$$N'(d) \cong 1 - \exp\{-N'N(d)\}.$$

The approximation is excellent when N' is large and $N(d)$ is small—say, $N' > 1{,}000$ and $N(d) < 1/N'$, as they are here. When $N(d) = 1/N'$, we have that $N'(d) \cong 1 - e^{-1} = 0.63$, which means that, with probability 0.63, a circle containing $1/N'$ of N contains at least one hard location. (On the average, the circle contains one location.) Solving for $N(d)$ in terms of $N'(d)$ gives

$$N(d) \cong -\ln[1 - N'(d)]/N',$$

from which we can compute percentiles of $N'(d)$:

$$N'^{-1}(p) \cong N^{-1}[-\ln(q)/N'],$$

where $0 \leq p \leq 1$ and $q = 1 - p$. For example, the median for the distance $d(x, x')$ is $N^{-1}[-\ln(0.5)/N']$. The normal distribution function with mean $n/2$ and standard deviation $\sqrt{n}/4$ can be used for $N(d)$. Selected points of the distribution $N'(d)$ are given in table 6.1.

As an example of a sparse memory, consider one with an address space $\{0, 1\}^{1{,}000}$ and with 1,000,000 hard locations: $N = \{0, 1\}^{1{,}000}$ and $N' = 1{,}000{,}000 \cong 2^{20}$. A hard location would then represent one millionth of the space, or 2^{980} addresses, on the average. A circle with a radius of 425

Table 6.1
Distribution of distance to nearest storage location, $N'(d)$, in a 1,000-dimensional memory with 1,000,000 locations.

d	$N'(d)$	z^a	$N(d)^b$
388.8	0.000001	−7.03	10^{-12}
394.0	0.00001	−6.71	10^{-11}
399.4	0.0001	−6.36	10^{-10}
405.2	0.001	−6.00	10^{-9}
411.3	0.01	−5.61	10^{-8}
417.9	0.1	−5.19	10^{-7}
421.0	0.25	−5.00	3×10^{-7}
423.7	0.5	−4.83	7×10^{-7}
425.9	0.75	−4.69	0.000001
427.6	0.9	−4.58	0.000002
429.9	0.99	−4.43	0.000005
431.3	0.999	−4.35	0.000007
432.2	0.9999	−4.28	0.000009
433.1	0.99999	−4.23	0.000012
433.7	0.999999	−4.19	0.000014

a. z is the number of standard deviations that d is below the mean distance 500: $z = (d - 500)/15.8$.
b. $N(d)$ is the distribution of the space N: $N(d) = \Pr\{d(x, y) \leq d\} \cong F(z)$.

bits contains a millionth of the space. From table 6.1 we see, for example, that the median distance to the nearest (hard) location is 424 bits (423.7, to be exact), and that only once in about 10,000 is the nearest location within 400 bits of a point. In 98 percent of the cases the distance from a point to the nearest hard location falls between 411 and 430 bits. In what follows, we will assume for simplicity that the distance from a *random* point of N to the hard location nearest to it is the median distance of 424 bits.

The Nearest-Neighbor Method in Sparse Memory

The rest of this chapter is an abortive attempt at using a sparse memory to solve the best-match problem. This attempt is included because it is the most obvious thing to try and because, as we will see in the next chapter, it fails for the very reason that distributed storage works.

Let X be a random data set of 10,000 words of $\{0, 1\}^{1,000}$. It is to be stored in a sparse memory that has 1,000,000 hard locations, and the object is to find the stored word that matches a test word the best.

The strategy most like the one used with the Best-Match Machine is to store each word ξ of X in the hard location nearest to ξ—namely, in ξ'. To

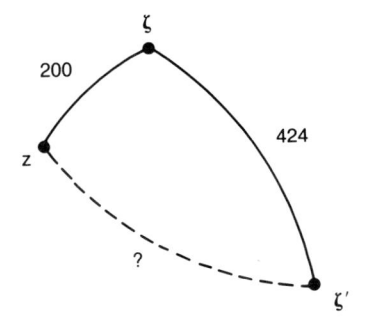

Figure 6.1
The distance from z to the location ζ', where the best-matching word ζ is stored. The "unknown" distance $d(z, \zeta')$ is approximately 454 bits.

find the best match to z, one would read the occupied hard location nearest to z. But that location would not, in general, contain the best match, or even a good match. In fact, storing ξ in the nearest hard location does not help much at all, as is shown by the following example.

Assume that the test word is z, that ζ is the element of X most similar to z, and that the distance between the two is 200 bits (which means that ζ is actually quite similar to z, so we would definitely want to find ζ; the parameter values of the example—1,000,000 locations, a 10,000-word data set, and $d(z, \zeta) = n/5 = 200$—have been selected with the later discussion of distributed storage in mind). There are two questions to ask: What is the probability that the occupied hard location nearest to z contains ζ (i.e., that the location in fact is ζ')? How similar to z, on the average, is the word of X contained in that location? (Notice that the location need not be z'—the hard location nearest to z—as z' can be empty.)

The word ζ has been stored in the location nearest to it, ζ' (which, according to the discussion at the end of the preceding section, is about 424 bits from ζ). Thus, we assume that $d(\zeta, \zeta') = 424$ bits; see figure 6.1. The average distance between z and ζ' is then given by the third side of the triangle $\{z, \zeta, \zeta'\}$ with known sides $\{z, \zeta\}$ and $\{\zeta, \zeta'\}$ as

$$d(z, \zeta') \cong 200 + 424 - 2 \cdot 200 \cdot 424/1{,}000 = 454 \text{ bits.}$$

We can expect to find approximately 0.0017 of N', or 1,700 hard locations, within 454 bits of z (0.001 of the space lies within 451 bits of a point according to table 1.2). About 0.01 of them, or 17 locations, are occupied by elements of X, and so, in a sense, ζ' is one of 17 locations. Its being the location nearest to z would therefore have a probability somewhere around 1/17,

$\Pr\{z'' = \zeta' | d(z, \zeta) = 200\} \cong 1/17,$

where z'' is the nearest X'-neighbor of z.

The probability of obtaining the best match with the nearest-neighbor method is low. In the example it is about 1/17—which, by the way, does not mean that examining the 17 occupied locations nearest to the test word z would guarantee that the best-matching word ζ would be found, although the probability of its being among the 17 is high. Nevertheless, it is reasonable to examine occupied locations in successively larger circles around z and compare their contents with z, although only rarely would the best match be guaranteed without the examining of at least half of memory (one need not look farther than twice the distance to the most similar word found so far).

The real weakness of the nearest-neighbor method becomes evident when data other than the addresses themselves are stored in memory— that is, if, instead of ζ, some other word η of N is stored in location ζ'. In terms introduced at the end of chapter 5, the data set then consists of pairs $\langle \xi, \eta \rangle$ instead of pairs $\langle \xi, \xi \rangle$, and for a test word z we want to find the word η that is paired with the ξ that matches z the best. The problem now is that the contents of location ξ' give no clue as to how close ξ is to z. Consequently, the probability of success in the example would be about 1/17, and there would be no way to tell by reading from memory whether the outcome is a success or a failure, or, in philosophers' terms, knowing whether one knows. (In the best-match case it is possible to tell.)

We can get an idea of how poor the method is (in 16 cases out of 17) by finding out how dissimilar are two addresses u and v that refer to the same hard location, that is, when $u' = v'$. Assume that $d(u, u') = d(v, u') = 424 \cong$ the median distance between a point of N and its nearest neighbor in N'. The mean length of the third side $\{u, v\}$ of the triangle $\{u, u', v\}$ is a good estimate of the distance $d(u, v)$. It is given by $2a(1 - a/n)$ (see "The Third Side of a Triangle" in chapter 1), and for $a = 424$ and $n = 1,000$ it is 488 bits, or a mere 0.75 standard deviation from the indifference distance (488 bits encompass slightly less than 1/4 of the space). This means that, as a rule, the contents of the nearest occupied location are unrelated to the retrieval cue.

I will conjecture that any simple method that either writes a word of the data set in just one location or reads from just one location of a sparse memory with preset addresses will not work. The reason is that the *contents of memory locations can be similar over sufficiently large, contiguous areas of N* (over 0.00001 of N, say) *only if they are similar over all of N*, that is, if they are essentially constant. This is a simple consequence of how the points of N are distributed: Any two points at indifference distance $n/2$ from each other have a common neighbor (in fact, many of them) that is very close to both in a probabilistic sense (the proportion of the space that lies within $n/4$ bits of a point is exceedingly small).

The following example demonstrates the above conclusion: Assume that the memory has 1,000-bit addresses ($n = 1,000$), that the contiguous areas are circles that cover but a billionth of the address space, and that the "similar" 1,000-bit words stored within any such circle differ from one another by at most 100 bits. The circles have a radius of 405 bits, according to table 1.2. If we now take an arbitrary address x and the union of the circles (with 405-bit radii) that include x, we get a circle of addresses with its center at x and with a radius of 810 bits. This larger circle includes almost all of the address space N (it excludes much less than a billionth), and the words stored within it differ from one another by at most 200 bits (since they differ from the word stored at x by at most 100 bits). The surface of a three-dimensional sphere fails to suggest this conclusion.

Chapter 7
Distributed Storage

The idea of distributed storage is that many storage locations participate in a single write or read operation—in marked contrast to conventional computer memories, in which only one location is active at once. Somewhat surprisingly, this gives the memory the appearance of a random-access memory with a very large address space and with data retrieved on the basis of similarity of address. More specifically, if the word η is stored at the address ξ, then reading from ξ retrieves η, and, what is more important, reading from an address x that is sufficiently similar to ξ retrieves a word y that is even more similar to η than x is to ξ (the similarities are comparable because the addresses to the memory and the data are elements of the same metric space, N).

The first of the postulates for sparse memory given at the beginning of chapter 6 stated that "the storage locations and their addresses are given from the start, and only the contents are modifiable." Nothing was said about the threshold that controls the range of addresses to which an address decoder responds. In chapter 6, as with the Best-Match Machine of chapter 5, the threshold was allowed to vary, and it provided the mechanism for searching memory for the nearest occupied location. With distributed storage, even the thresholds of the address decoders can be fixed. This simplifies the construction of the memory further, leaving the contents of the locations as the only things that need to be modified.

The mathematical feasibility of distributed storage is the main result of this study. It will be demonstrated first with reference to the problem of the best match, but the result applies in general. We shall also have occasion to estimate the capacity of the memory, that is, the maximum number of words that can be stored successfully in a memory of a given size (meaning that the words can be retrieved later). Certain properties of the data retrieved from memory can be interpreted as the philosophers' notion of knowing that one knows, and certain states of a search as the psychologists' notion of a tip-of-the-tongue state. Such interpretations are given at the end of this chapter.

62   Chapter 7

Concepts Related to Distributed Storage

In what follows, frequent reference will be made to an example of a sparse memory with a thousand dimensions and a million hard locations ($n = 1{,}000$ and $N' = 1{,}000{,}000$). The following notation will be used: Words of the data set stored in the memory will be designated by letters of the Greek alphabet. The only other use of the Greek letters is for addresses used in writing (i.e., for centers of write circles—to be discussed in this chapter). Latin letters will stand for general points of the (address) space N. When appropriate, z will stand for a test word and ζ for the target word (the word of the data set most similar to z—the one for zeroing in).

Access Radius, r, and Access Circle, $O'(x)$ We shall require that when the memory is addressed with x, the locations closest to x are accessed. More specifically, all the locations within a given distance r of x will either store or provide data, depending on whether the memory is being written into or read from. This defines the access circle $O'(r, x)$ as the hard locations in the circle $O(r, x)$. Since the access radius r will be constant throughout the discussion, it is convenient to abbreviate $O(r, x)$ to $O(x)$ and $O'(r, x)$ to $O'(x)$. The access circle then is the (multi)set of hard locations given by

$$O'(x) = N' \cap O(x).$$

We say that the (hard) location y' is *accessible* from x if y' is no farther than r bits from x—that is, if y' is in the access circle $O'(x)$. In our example, assume that $1/1{,}000$ of N (and of N' on the average) is accessed at once. A circle with a radius of 451 bits covers $1/1{,}000$ of the space (see table 1.2), and so the access radius $r_{0.001}$ is 451 bits. The mean number of hard locations in an access circle is then $1{,}000$.

Most locations in the access circle are quite far from the center of the circle. The location closest to the center is 424 bits from the center, on the average (the median distance to the nearest location is 423.7 bits according to table 6.1). The average (median) distance from the center to the 1,000 or so locations of the access circle is 448 bits (a circle with 448-bit radius encloses 0.0005 of the space according to table 1.2), which is only three bits short of the maximum distance of 451 bits.

Access Overlap, $I'(x, y)$ The set of hard locations accessible from both x and y is given by

$$I'(x, y) = O'(x) \cap O'(y).$$

The mean number of locations in this access overlap depends on the size of the access circle and on the distance $d(x, y)$ between the centers of the

Table 7.1
Mean number of hard locations in access overlap of two circles with radii $r_{0.001} = 451$ in a 1,000-dimensional memory with 1,000,000 locations.

d^a	Number of locations	d	Number of locations	d	Number of locations	d	Number of locations	d	Number of locations
0	1000	21	619	60	400	160	146	360	13
1	894	23	603	65	376	170	132	370	11
2	894	25	588	70	361	180	119	380	10
3	842	27	573	75	339	190	107	390	8
4	842	29	559	80	326	200	97	400	7
5	803	31	546	85	307	210	87	410	6
6	803	33	533	90	295	220	78	420	5
7	770	35	521	95	277	230	70	430	4
8	770	37	509	100	267	240	62	440	4
9	743	39	497	105	251	250	55	450	3
10	743	41	486	110	241	260	49	460	2
11	718	43	475	115	228	270	44	470	2
12	718	45	465	120	219	280	39	480	2
13	695	47	455	125	206	290	34	490	1
14	695	49	445	130	198	300	30	500	1
15	674	51	435	135	186	310	26	510	1
16	674	53	426	140	179	320	23	520	1
17	655	55	417	145	169	330	20	530	0
18	655	57	408	150	162	340	18	540	0
19	636	59	400	155	152	350	15	550	0

a. d is the distance, in bits, between the centers of the two circles.

overlapping circles, as figure 1.2 suggests. Table 7.1 gives this number for our sample memory, and figure 7.1 shows it graphically. The outstanding fact is that, for the values of r that interest us here, the size of the overlap falls rapidly as the distance between the centers increases.

Contents of a Location, $C(x')$ We need to specify what a storage location will contain. Let us start with the generous assumption that it can contain the multiset of all the words that have ever been written in it. This is a drastic departure from computer memories in which the old word in a location is replaced by a newly written word. We shall postpone questions of how to construct memory locations of unlimited capacity, both because it is easier to develop the theory when we assume unlimited capacity and because in the end we make do with a relatively small capacity.

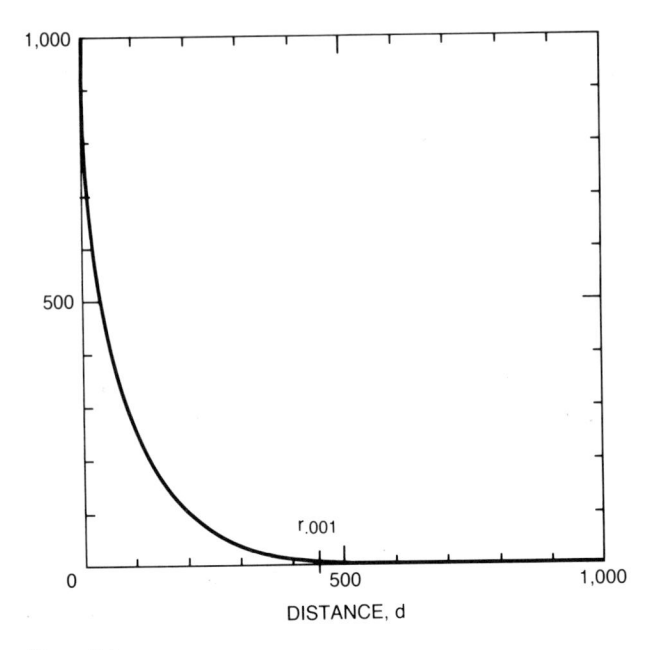

Figure 7.1
Mean number of hard locations in the access overlap of table 7.1 as a function of the distance between the centers of the two circles.

Writing in x'   Writing the word η in hard location x' means including it in the multiset of words $C(x')$ contained in x',

$$C(x') := C(x') \uplus [\eta].$$

Writing with Address ξ, or Writing at ξ   Writing the word η at ξ means writing η in all the (hard) locations accessible from ξ. All told, $|O'(\xi)|$ copies of η are stored in memory. In the example, η is written in the approximately 1,000 locations closest to ξ.

Data at x, $D(x)$ The data *at* x are the pooled contents of the locations accessible from x (i.e., the multiunion of the contents):

$$D(x) = \biguplus_{y' \in O'(x)} C(y').$$

These are the words retrieved by reading with the address x.

Two comments must be made about the pooled data $D(x)$: First, if the word η has been written with the address ξ, the multiset $D(x)$ contains $|O'(x) \cap O'(\xi)|$ copies of η, one from each location accessible from both x and ξ (see figure 7.2). Second, most of the words in $D(x)$ have been written

STORAGE LOCATIONS

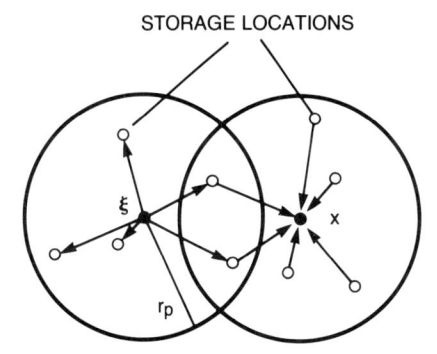

Figure 7.2
Writing at ξ and reading at x.

with addresses quite dissimilar to x. In our example, most of them have been written with addresses that are more than 488 bits from x (12 bits short of the indifference distance, which is less than one standard deviation), as can be shown by a calculation identical to the one on page 58. A similar calculation applied to the 448-bit median distance from the center of an access circle to the locations in the circle (see p. 62) gives 494 bits as a *typical* distance from the center of the read circle to the centers of the write circles that contribute to the pooled data.

Reading at x   Reading at x means taking a representative (an element of N) of the data at x. The selection of the representative is a statistical problem that will be dealt with in the next section.

Word at x   The word at x, $W(x)$, is a properly chosen representative of the data at x. It is what reading at x yields.

The Feasibility of Distributed Storage: Finding the Best Match

The feasibility of distributed storage is shown by showing that a sequence of successively read words converges in the right way. This is done most easily with reference the best-match problem by showing that the convergence is to the best-matching word of the data set. We will see that the conditions for convergence are (1) that not too many words have been stored in memory and (2) that the first reading address (i.e., the test pattern) is sufficiently close to the address with which the target word was written (i.e., the target pattern).

To our earlier assumptions, $n = 1{,}000$, $N' = 1{,}000{,}000$, and $r = r_{0.001} = 451$, we add the assumption that the data set X has 10,000 words. Since each write operation adds a word to each of about 1,000 locations, storing the entire data set means that some 10^7 words are stored in memory, or an average of 10 words per location. This gives our first estimate for the capacity of a storage location: A location should be able to store at least 10 words. Reading will pool the data of about 1,000 locations, yielding a multiset D of about 10,000 words. To summarize: $|X| = 10,000$, $|O'(x)| \cong 1,000$, $|C(x')| \cong 10$, and $|D(x)| \cong 10,000$ (x is a random point of N).

For the problem of the best match, storing the data set X is analogous to storing it in the Best-Match Machine of chapter 5; that is, the word ξ of X is written at ξ. But instead of one copy of ξ being stored, 1,000 copies are—one in each location accessible from ξ. After the entire data set has been stored, location x' will contain the multiset of words of X that are accessible from x', or

$$C(x') = X \cap O(x').$$

Representative of the Pooled Data, $W(x)$ Assume that the test word is z and that the word of X most similar to z is ζ. We start by reading at z, which means that the contents of the locations accessible from z are pooled into the multiset of data $D(z)$. How should the representative of $D(z)$ be chosen? I will describe three possible methods first and then settle on a fourth.

The first method would be to examine each element of $D(z)$ and take the one *most similar to* z. It guarantees success if the best-matching word of X is similar to z (say, within 200 bits of it). However, the method can be dismissed on two grounds: First, the pooled data $D(z)$ will be very large. In our example, $D(z)$ will have as many words as the data set X itself, so that nothing would be gained by storing the data set in a random-access memory. Second, the method does not generalize beyond the best-match problem—that is, to cases in which a word unrelated to ζ is written at ζ—because the contents of a location would then bear no relation to the location's address.

The remaining three methods are statistical and are based on the *frequency* of words in the multiset of pooled data. The number of copies of the word ξ in the pooled data $D(z)$ is given by the size of the access overlap when writing at ξ and then reading at z; therefore, it is $|O'(z) \cap O'(\xi)|$. (See figure 7.2, and remember that ξ has been written at ξ.) The closer the circle centers z and ξ are to each other, the more the circles overlap (see figure 7.1). Thus, if ζ is the word of X most similar to z, we can expect ζ to be the most frequent word in the pooled data $D(z)$. Reading at z in the second, third, and fourth methods is then done by taking, respectively, the most frequent word of the pooled data, a random word of the pooled data, and a word of N that is an archetype of the pooled data.

Taking the *most frequent word* in $D(z)$ is sound in principle, but the

Distributed Storage 67

computational task of deciding which 1,000-bit word is most frequent among some 10,000 words seems insurmountable. This second method is therefore judged to be impractical.

In the third method we would take a *random word* of the pooled data $D(z)$. But notice that the 10,000 or so words of $D(z)$ contain at most about 1,000 copies of ζ (if $z = \zeta$). If the distance from z to ζ is 200 bits, there are only about 95 copies of ζ among the 10,000 (see table 7.1). Thus, the probability of selecting at random the right element would be no more than 1/10, and usually it would be much less (it would be about 1/100 if $d(z, \zeta) = 200$).

The second and third methods appear to require that the words be stored intact in the memory locations; that is, they do not seem amenable to compressed forms of storage. This drawback is overcome by the fourth method.

The fourth and final method is to compute an element of N that is an *archetype* of the pooled data $D(z)$ but not necessarily an element of it. A natural candidate is an average of the words of $D(z)$. The simplest average is obtained by applying the *majority rule* to each bit, or coordinate, independently of the others. This average is the best representative of $D(z)$ in the sense that it is the word of N with the smallest mean distance to the words of $D(z)$. *Reading at z* henceforth refers to *taking the average of the pooled data $D(z)$*.

The ith bit of the average is given by summing over the ith bits of the words in the pooled data and then thresholding with half the size of the pooled data:

$$W_i(z) = 1 \text{ iff } \sum_{\xi \in D(z)} \xi_i \geq |D(z)|/2.$$

Notice that only sums—and not the individual words—are needed to compute the average word. This simplifies greatly the construction of the memory, as we will see later.

The above bit sum can be written as

$$\sum_{\xi \in D(z)} \xi_i = \sum_{\xi \in X} |O'(z) \cap O'(\xi)| \xi_i$$

to show that the size of the overlap of the write and read circles serves as a weight in computing the average. It is by virtue of such weighting that the element of X most frequent in $D(z)$, and hence most similar to z, might be recovered.

The average of the pooled data, as defined above, is a satisfactory representative of the data so long as the words written in memory are a random sample of N, in which case zeros and ones are equally probable. This assumption is not necessary for the development of the theory, but for simplicity we will adhere to it in the remainder of this chapter.

Convergence to the Best-Matching Word Under the proper conditions, a sequence of words read from memory starting with the address z converges to the word ζ of X that matches z the best. Specifically, the memory is first read at z to obtain the word $z(1)$; it is then read at $z(1)$ to obtain the word $z(2)$, and so forth, generating the sequence of words $z(0), \ldots, z(i), \ldots$, where $z(0) = z$ and $z(i) = W(z(i-1))$ for $i = 1, 2, \ldots$. This manner of reading is called *iterated reading starting at z*.

What happens when we read at ζ if we have previously written the word ζ at ζ? Can we recover ζ? When the word ζ was written, one copy of it was written in each of the locations in the access circle $O'(\zeta)$, for a total of about 1,000 copies. Reading at ζ retrieves all of them but also about 10,000 copies of words other than ζ. (Reading at a previously written address retrieves about 11,000 words, whereas reading at a random address retrieves about 10,000 words.) However, the other words come mostly in ones or in very small groups, because the intersection of the read circle $O'(\zeta)$ with the write circle $O'(x)$, for most x in N (and in X), is about 0.001 of $O'(\zeta)$, or just one hard location. Against such background noise, the weight of 1,000 is sufficient for the retrieval of ζ (or for its reconstruction, whichever way one wants to look at the computing of the average).

A detailed analysis of the average is given in appendix C. The statistics for a single bit of the average (say, the ith coordinate) work out as follows: The data set X has 9,999 words other than ζ. Each of them occurs once, on the average, in the approximately 10,000 words of the pooled data $D(\zeta)$, and hence their ith coordinates resemble 10,000 Bernoulli trials with a 0.5 probability of an outcome's being 0 (or 1). The sum of such trials has a mean of 5,000 and a standard deviation of 50. Adding to it 1,000 copies of the ith bit of ζ brings the mean sum to 5,500. It is 5,000 if the bit is 0 and 6,000 if it is 1. So we will be measuring a 500-unit deviation from the mean with a standard deviation of 50, which makes the probability of guessing the bit correctly not less than $1 - 1/10^{22}$. The probability of guessing all 1,000 bits correctly and thus retrieving ζ is then the 1,000th power of that, $(1 - 1/10^{22})^{1,000} \cong 1 - 1/10^{19}$, or a near certainty, allowing us to say that the word recovered by reading at ζ indeed is ζ, or $W(\zeta) = \zeta$.

Next consider the problem of finding, for a test word z, the word ζ of X that is most similar to z (i.e., finding the best match). Assume that the distance $d(z, \zeta)$ between the two is 200 bits. The claim is that reading at z yields a word that is closer to ζ than z is. The word ζ now has a weight of $|O'(z) \cap O'(\zeta)|$, which, according to table 7.1, is about 97. The 10,000 or so other words of X, again, have a weight of about 1 each. By an argument similar to the one above, we will be measuring a 48.5-unit deviation from the mean with a standard deviation of 50. A bit of the read word $W(z)$ will then match the corresponding bit of ζ with probability 0.83, and the expected distance from $W(z)$ to ζ will be $1,000 - 830 = 170$ bits, or 30

Table 7.2
Transformation of distance to target by reading with access radius $r_{0.001}$ from a 1,000-dimensional memory with 1,000,000 locations after 10,000 write operations.

Distance							
Old	New	Old	New	Old	New	Old	New
0	0	180	135	250	305	400	474
70	0	185	148	260	325	410	478
80	1	190	160	270	344	420	482
90	3	195	173	280	361	430	485
100	7	200	186	290	376	440	487
110	12	205	199	300	391	450	489
120	21	<u>209</u>	<u>209</u>	310	404	460	491
130	33	210	212	320	416	470	493
140	48	215	224	330	426	480	494
150	67	220	236	340	436	490	495
155	77	225	249	350	444	500	496
160	87	230	260	360	452	520	498
165	99	235	272	370	458	540	499
170	110	240	283	380	464	560	499
175	123	245	294	390	470	580	500

bits less than the original distance 200. Repeating the procedure with $W(z)$ gives $W(W(z))$, which is but 100 bits from ζ, and two more iterations suffice to reproduce ζ. (The next distance to ζ would be about 4 bits, and the one after that zero.)

Table 7.2 shows how the new distance to the target, $d(W(z), \zeta)$, depends on the old distance, $d(z, \zeta)$. A slightly more accurate (and larger) estimate of the variance of a bit sum has been used in computing this table (the variance is derived in appendix C), and so the values in the table are not exactly the same as those in the previous paragraph. Figure 7.3 plots the data of table 7.2.

Iterated reading fails to converge to the best-matching word if the original distance, $d(z, \zeta)$, is too large. In the example, a test word more than 210 bits from the target will not, as a rule, find its target. For example, according to table 7.2, $d(z, \zeta) = 220$ yields $d(W(z), \zeta) = 236$, which yields $d(W(W(z)), \zeta) = 274$, which yields $d(W(W(W(z))), \zeta) = 350$, which yields ... $\cong 500$, and so this sequence diverges. (Notice that these values, as well as those given two paragraphs above, are rounded mean values and thus give only a general idea of how an actual sequence might converge or diverge.) Converging and diverging sequences are illustrated in figure 7.4.

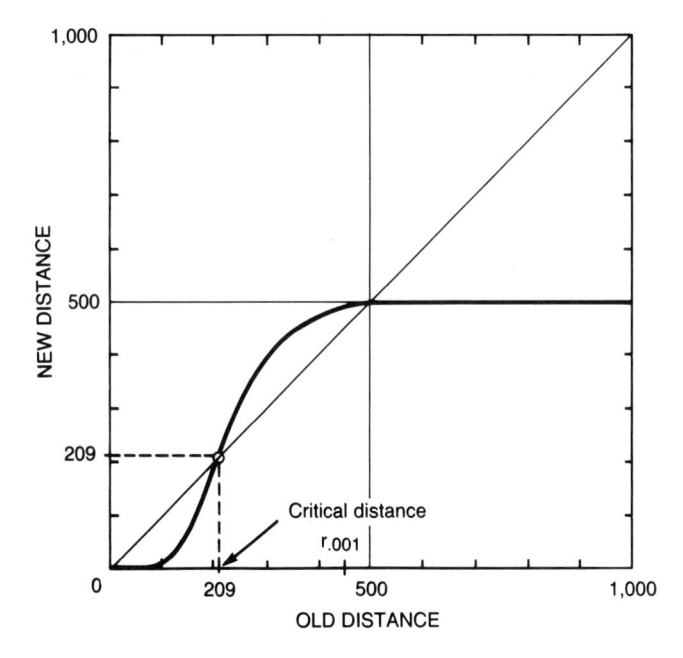

Figure 7.3
New distance to target as a function of old distance.

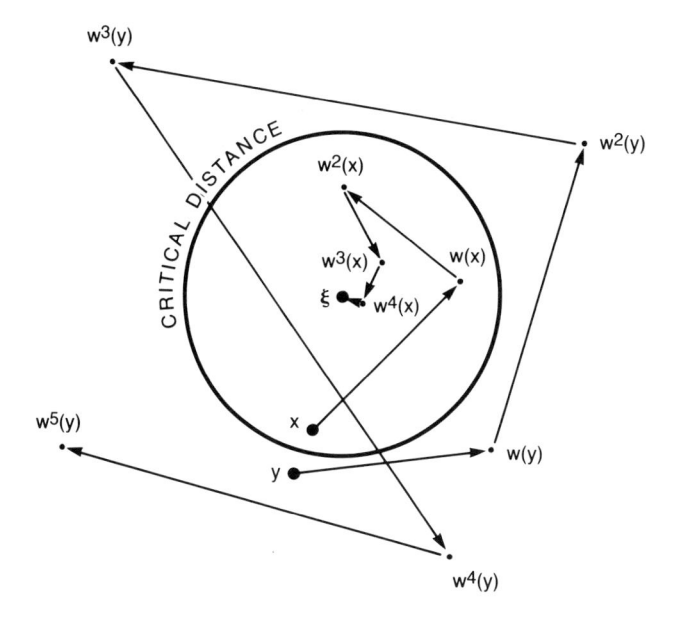

Figure 7.4
Converging and diverging sequences.

Further Concepts and Properties of Distributed Storage

The key properties of distributed storage have been demonstrated here with reference to data of the form $\langle \xi, \xi \rangle$, meaning that the word ξ is written at ξ. They will be summarized and further amplified below. More general forms of data will be discussed in the next chapter.

Signal Strength Signal strength is defined here as the weight of the target word ζ in the pooled data $D(z)$ obtained by reading at z. It equals the size of the overlap of the read circle with the target write circle, $|O'(z) \cap O'(\zeta)|$. Signal strength as a function of the distance between the read address and the target address is shown in table 7.1. Maximum signal strength (obtained by reading at the write address, $z = \zeta$) is the number of locations in the access circle (approximately pN', where p is the portion of the space covered by the access circle). The maximum signal strength of the example is 1,000. The average signal strength is $p^2 N'$ ($= 1$ in the example). Notice that writing a given word k times at a given address results in a k-fold signal strength for that word.

Noise Noise is defined here as the standard deviation of the ith bit-sum in the data pooled at a random point of N. In the example its value is 50. In appendix C, where different but equivalent definitions of writing and reading are used (the values for signal and noise there are twice what they are above), noise is approximately $\sqrt{p^2 N' T}$, where T is the size of the data set that has been stored in memory. The ratio of signal strength to noise, or simply the signal-to-noise ratio, is a normalized quantity. It will be denoted by R. The maximum signal-to-noise ratio, in the terms of appendix C, is therefore

$$R_{\max} \cong \frac{pN'}{\sqrt{p^2 N' T}}$$
$$= \sqrt{N'/T}.$$

Whenever this ratio is high enough (in the example of the previous section it is 10), a word written at ξ is recovered, with high probability, by reading at or near ξ.

Fidelity Fidelity at z, denoted by P, is defined here as the probability that a bit of the read word, $W(z)$, matches that of the target word, ζ. From this definition it follows that

$$P = \Pr\{W_i(z) = \zeta_i\}$$
$$\cong F(R),$$

where F is the normal distribution function. The probability that $W(z)$ is the target word is then the nth power of fidelity.

Maximum fidelity is obtained by reading at the target address. In the example, the fidelity at 200 bits from the target is 0.83 and the maximum fidelity is somewhere around $1 - 1/10^{22}$. The quantity $1 - P$ tells us how far, on the average, the read word $W(z)$ is from the target. This relation has been given in table 7.2 and figure 7.3. Wherever in figure 7.3 the function is below the 45° line, the read word $W(z)$ is closer to the target, on the average, than is the original word z.

Convergence and Divergence The convergence of a sequence of successively read words is the key property of distributed storage. It means that the current estimate of the target word can be improved by reading from memory. It also means that successively read words get closer and closer to one another until they are identical. The stationary condition for a *divergent* sequence is characterized by adjacent words' being approximately orthogonal to one another (and to the target). By chance, an initially diverging sequence can converge to a random word of the data set X. Such convergence (which will be called *chance convergence*) is characterized by a very long expected time to convergence.

Critical Distance A sequence of read words converges only if the initial address is sufficiently close to the target. The distance beyond which divergence is more likely than convergence will be called the *critical distance*. In the example it is 209 bits (see table 7.2). As more words are stored in memory, the critical distance decreases until it reaches zero, and thereafter it vanishes, meaning that stored words are no longer retrievable (nowhere is there convergence).

The critical distance is the distance at which there is probability 0.5 that the word read from memory is closer to the target word than the reading address is. A very good estimate of the critical distance can be obtained by finding the distance at which the arithmetic mean of the new distance to the target equals the old distance to the target—that is, by solving $1 - P(d) = d/n$ for d, where $P(d)$ is fidelity as a function of distance. This distance is indicated in figure 7.3 by the intersection of the distance function with the 45° line at $d = 209$ bits.

Rates of Convergence and Divergence When the reading address is at about the critical distance from the target, the probability of getting closer to the target by reading from memory is about 0.5. Successively read words can then bounce back and forth and remain at about the critical distance for some time. However, once the distance to the target differs clearly from

Table 7.3
Distance between two read chains in reading with access radius $r_{0.001}$ from a 1,000-dimensional memory.

Old distance	New distance	R[a]
0	0	1.00
1	132	0.92
2	157	0.88
5	199	0.81
10	237	0.74
20	283	0.63
50	355	0.44
100	415	0.26
200	470	0.09
500	500	0.00

a. R is the correlation of the bit sums corresponding to the old distance.

the critical distance, convergence to the target or divergence to random indifferent points is rapid (fewer than ten iterations, as a rule).

In contrast, the expected time of chance convergence is extremely long. In the example, the probability that a random point of N is within the critical distance of 209 bits of the nearest point of X is something like 10^{-50}, and so the expected time of chance convergence to some point of X is somewhere around 10^{50} iterations. Therefore, the comparison of adjacent terms of a sequence soon reveals whether the sequence will converge or (initially) diverge. These very long times to chance convergence are possible only with very large memories and proportionally large data sets written in them. With small memories and data sets, starting at a random point results in a relatively rapid convergence to a point or a cycle.

We have seen that reading near a previously written address brings us closer to the target address. It is instructive to see how the words found by reading at two nearby addresses compare with one another when the addresses are far from any previously written address. This corresponds to reading at two random points of $\{0, 1\}^n$ that are near each other. The result is that the two sequences are orthogonal to one another after only two or three read iterations. For the sample memory, this is seen in table 7.3; if, for example, the initial reading addresses are but one bit apart, the words that are read are 132 bits apart, on the average. Further reading with the addresses that are 132 bits apart yields a pair of words that are over 430 bits apart, on the average, and one more reading yields a pair of words that are orthogonal to one another. (Table 7.3 is derived in appendix D.)

Table 7.4
Capacity of sparse distributed memory with N' storage locations.

n (number of dimensions)	c (capacity as a multiple of N')	$1/c$
100	0.165	6.1
200	0.137	7.3
500	0.112	9.0
1,000	0.098	10.2
2,000	0.087	11.5
5,000	0.076	13.2
10,000	0.069	14.5
20,000	0.063	15.8
50,000	0.057	17.6
100,000	0.053	18.9

Memory Capacity Memory capacity is defined here as the size of the data set for which the critical distance is zero. A memory filled to capacity is said to be *full*, and a memory filled beyond capacity is said to be *overloaded*. If the word ξ has been written at ξ in a full memory, the probability of reading ξ at ξ is, by definition, 0.5. In an overloaded memory the probability is less than 0.5. In either case, if the memory is read at a point x just one bit from ξ, the probability of reading ξ is quite small, and a sequence of successively read words diverges rapidly.

Memory capacity can now be estimated by setting the nth power of the maximum fidelity to $\frac{1}{2}$ and solving for T. From

$$[F(\sqrt{N'/T})]^n = \tfrac{1}{2}$$

we get the capacity

$$T = N'/H(n),$$

where $H(n) = [F^{-1}(1/2^{1/n})]^2$. Thus, the capacity is proportional to the number of hard locations N'. For $n = 1,000$ we have $H(n) = 10.22 \cong 10$, so the capacity in our example is about one-tenth the number of hard locations. Table 7.4 gives memory capacity as a fraction of the number of hard locations N' for selected values of n. The capacity of the sample memory, with its 1,000,000 hard locations, is slightly less than 100,000.

Capacity of a Storage Location We can now get an idea of how many words a single location must store. Filling memory beyond capacity means that words that have been written only once can no longer be retrieved. They are forgotten because of increased noise. It therefore seems unneces-

Distributed Storage   75

sary for storage locations to have a larger capacity than is needed to fill the memory to near capacity. How much is that?

If a memory of N' locations is filled to its capacity T and if the access radius is r_p, the total number of words in memory is about TpN', and the average number per location is TpN'/N', which equals pT. For $n = 1,000$ and for p small, the capacity is somewhat less than $N'/10$, so let us use $T = N'/10$. A location of a full memory would then contain about $pN'/10$ words. In our example, that would be 100 words. Recall that the average word of the pooled data can be computed from n bit-sums. Therefore, a bit location can be realized as a counter that is incremented by 1 to store 1 and decremented by 1 to store 0. If zeros and ones are equally probable, the mean sum will be zero and the standard deviation will be $\sqrt{pT}$. For the sample memory, the standard deviation is $\sqrt{100} = 10$, and so a bit location that can store the integers $-40, \ldots, 40$ will suffice (only occasionally will it overflow before the memory is full). The range of values can be reduced to perhaps as little as $-10, \ldots, 10$ by reducing the size of the write circle and by not attempting to fill the memory to capacity. This would guarantee convergence for all recently stored items, as the following example shows.

When the capacity of a location is limited, the location will eventually overflow. This means that there is an attempt to increment a bit counter that has reached its maximum value or to decrement one that has reached its minimum value. Let us assume that in such cases the counter remains unchanged. It is interesting to see how such a memory performs.

I will discuss only the extreme case in which a bit counter has but two values: 0 and 1. Writing a 0 decrements the count to 0; writing a 1 increments it to 1. In other words, a bit location stores only the last bit written, just as it does in a conventional computer memory. The difference is that writing a word now stores it in more than one location (in about 1,000 locations in our example).

Assume that the word ξ is written at ξ and that immediately thereafter the memory is read at ξ. The 1,000 or so copies of ξ are retrieved, and nothing else, and no doubt the word read would be ξ. If instead the memory is read at another address, x, then

$$|O'(x) \cap O'(\xi)|$$

copies of ξ are read, together with about

$$1,000 - |O'(x) \cap O'(\xi)|$$

words other than ξ. By a method used for the best-match problem, we can estimate that the signal strength is

$$|O'(x) \cap O'(\xi)|/2,$$

the noise is

$$\sqrt{(1{,}000 - |O'(x) \cap O'(\xi)|) \cdot \tfrac{1}{2} \cdot \tfrac{1}{2}},$$

and the critical distance to ξ is about 380 bits, meaning that a word just written would be read easily. However, subsequent writing will replace the 1,000 copies of ξ as follows: A location survives one write operation with probability $q = 1 - p$ ($= 0.999$), and so the probability that it survives T write operations is q^T. Signal strength for the word ξ after T write operations is then q^T times the original signal strength, or

$$q^T |O'(x) \cap O'(\xi)|/2.$$

In our example this means that when ξ is 2,300 write operations "old," reading at ξ retrieves ξ with probability 0.5 (the critical distance to ξ has been reduced to zero).

In accordance with our definition of memory capacity, we might say that this memory has a capacity of 2,300 words. Notice, however, that much younger words are retrieved readily. For example, the critical distance to a word that is 1,000 write operations old is about 240 bits. A similar calculation shows that reducing the access radius from $r_{0.001}$ to $r_{0.0001}$ increases the capacity to about 11,400 words. A word would then be written in about 100 locations. Reducing the radius much below that would increase the capacity further but would reduce the critical distance, even for newly written words, to such a low value as to do away with useful convergence. As the access circle decreases, the storage scheme begins to resemble that in the nearest-neighbor method in sparse memory, which was criticized in chapter 6.

In this memory, forgetting is caused by gradual loss of signal strength in addition to increased noise, because here new data replace old.

Interpretations

Certain properties of the memory model could be interpreted as counterparts of psychological phenomena. They are not necessarily unique to this memory model, but they are illustrated clearly by it.

Fast convergence—fewer than ten memory reads versus endless millions—could be used as an indication of knowing that one knows. That is, one can start with a retrieval cue, and immediately the successively read words begin to get closer to one another. If one looks at a single bit, it settles down, whereas if the sequence diverges, the bit behaves randomly with each new read.

Related to this is the tip-of-the-tongue state, or the feeling that one is close to recalling an item. The model has something corresponding to it, namely, being about the critical distance (209 bits in the example) from the nearest stored item. At that point the rate of convergence is slow.

The memory provides another internal measure of distance to the target: the magnitudes of the pooled bit sums. When the read address is near the target address, these sums are far from their mean values, and vice versa. A circuit that measures deviations of the bit sums from their means is realized easily with neurons, although its construction is not pursued here. The output of such a circuit could be interpreted as the subjective feeling of knowing how close to the target one is.

Rehearsal (e.g., piano practicing) would write an item many times in memory and so would increase its signal strength and hence the critical distance to that item. A well-rehearsed item would therefore be retrieved with fewer retrieval cues than an item stored only once.

A full or overloaded memory could support momentary feelings of familiarity that would fade away rapidly, as if one could not maintain attention.

If the capacity of storage locations is sufficiently small, the memory could never be filled to capacity, and the most recently stored items could always be retrieved. Forgetting would increase with the length of time (i.e., the number of intervening write operations) that an item has been stored in memory.

Distributed storage could explain the nonspecific effects of brain damage. There can be noticeable physical damage with little apparent effect on performance. If the damage is extensive but not total in any critical area, the effect is the lowering of the general level of performance rather than a total loss of particular abilities (or memories). This could be explained by the fact that copies of each memory item are stored in multiple locations. The distribution of the space $\{0, 1\}^n$ is such that, no matter how the locations are arranged physically in a three-dimensional space, the ones within $r_{0.001}$ bits of a reference address (in n-dimensional space) cannot, as a rule, be in any one restricted region of the three-dimensional space, but are distributed all over it. Reduction in the number of locations N' (the death of neurons) reduces the critical distance for all stored items, so that increasingly exact cues are needed to recognize or recall stored items.

Chapter 8
Storage and Retrieval of Sequences: Predicting

This chapter is concerned with the learning of sequences. We seek to answer the question of how information should be stored in memory so that it can be retrieved later when the situation warrants it. This requires two things: that the *present* situation be recognized as being *similar to* some situation in the *past* and that the *consequences* of that past situation be retrieved.

Let us start by looking at a possible source of confusion about the memory itself. The best-match problem requires that the word ξ be written at ξ, and, consequently, the memory behaves as if it were content addressable. But in fact it is no more so than is the conventional random-access memory of a computer. For other kinds of problems we would store some other word η at ξ, and to retrieve η the memory would have to be addressed with ξ. Addressing it with η, which is the contents, would retrieve neither ξ nor η.

Because of the unifying principle (i.e., contents of memory can be used to address the memory), the memory might be thought of as content addressable in a more general sense. But then, so would an ordinary computer memory, for there, too, memory locations can contain addresses of other locations. Therefore, the sparse distributed memory really is a random-access memory, and how it behaves in any particular instance depends on *where* the data are stored. For example, if a sequence of words is stored as a pointer chain, the memory can support sequential accessing. Any word in the sequence can then be retrieved (by addressing memory with the previous word in the sequence), and the remaining sequence can be retrieved by reading from memory repeatedly. In this way, time can be included in the memory trace, whereas it is not at all clear how to store sequences in a truly content-addressable memory.

General Data Storage

Consider the data set (a multiset) of T address-datum pairs (random elements of $N \times N$),

$$X = [\langle \xi_t, \eta_t \rangle | t = 0, \ldots, T - 1],$$

which is stored in memory by writing the word η_t at ξ_t. Assume that T is well below the capacity of the memory—say, $T = 10{,}000$ and $N' = 1{,}000{,}000$, as in the preceding chapter. The definitions and properties discussed in the preceding chapter carry over with one exception: Successively read words do not, as a rule, converge to a single word. Say that we read at ξ_t. By statistical arguments identical to the ones in the preceding chapter, η_t is retrieved, or $W(\xi_t) = \eta_t$, with near certainty. But if we then read at η_t, a random word of N is retrieved—unless, of course, η_t happens to equal (or to be very similar to) the address part of some pair in X.

In this context, convergence means the following: If ξ_t is the write address most similar to x and if x is sufficiently similar to ξ_t (within the critical distance) but not equal to ξ_t, then the word $W(x)$ read at x is *more* similar to the word η_t written at ξ_t than x is to ξ_t, or

$$E\{d(W(x), \eta_t)\} < d(x, \xi_t).$$

On the other hand, if the read address, x, differs enough from the closest write address, ξ_t—by well over 209 bits in the example—the distance between what is read at x and what was written at ξ_t tends toward the indifference distance—in symbols, critical distance $< d(x, \xi_t) < n/2$ implies that

$$d(x, \xi_t) < E\{d(W(x), \eta_t)\} < n/2.$$

The amount by which a single reading transforms distance is the same here as it is in the best-match data (see table 7.2 and figure 7.3).

Storage of Sequences

Background Assume that an organism's experience is represented by a finite sequence of events and is encoded as a sequence of memory items. How should such a sequence be stored in memory, and how should it be retrieved so as to be of value to the organism? By something's being of value to an organism, I mean that it allows the organism to predict (and to act accordingly; appropriate behavior entails successful prediction). At the very least, the ability to predict helps the organism to survive in a changing environment.

The key to successful prediction is the ability to make use of the past; that is, to make use of regularities in the sequence that represents the organism's experience. The function of memory is then to make *relevant information* available *rapidly enough*. The relevance of the information depends on the situation, and "rapidly enough" means that it is possible to act on the information before the opportunity has passed. Put another way, the more rapidly some information is made available to an organism, the more opportunities there are for the organism to exploit. Thus, speed is important.

The present is predicted best by the most recent past and by earlier events similar to it. If event A is usually followed by event B—that is, if the transition $\langle A, B \rangle$ has been common in the organism's past—the organism should learn to expect B (or a B-like event) whenever A (or an A-like event) has just happened. This tells us that the memory item for B should be stored in such a way that when the memory is cued with A, B is retrieved. A random-access memory can support such retrieval by storing the word B in location A, or, in computer jargon, by having A point to B. Of course, we need to assume that an event, or rather the corresponding memory item, can address memory. And this we do assume.

The simple idea that A helps to retrieve B is behind the associative-strength models of memory. Such models seem to arise from logical necessity. Formalisms for their study include Markov processes and mathematical learning theory (stimulus-response theory). We shall see that our generalized random-access memory provides a mechanism for realizing simple Markov models.

To sum up: The memory should allow the present situation to act as a retrieval cue, and, when presented with a situation that is *similar* to some previously encountered situation, it should retrieve the *consequences* of that previous situation. This highly significant observation is already explicit in Marr 1969 (p. 464). I will now develop these ideas more rigorously.

Storing Transitions in Memory Let the first T moments of an organism's experience be represented by a sequence of length T of n-bit words,

$$X(T) = \langle \xi_0, \ldots, \xi_{T-1} \rangle \text{ for } T = 0, 1, 2, \ldots.$$

The sequence $X(T)$ is called the organism's *past* at time T. Notice that $X(T)$ is an element of $[\{0, 1\}^n]^T$, or of N^T for short.

A (first-order) *transition* $\langle \xi_{t-1}, \xi_t \rangle$, where $t = 1, \ldots, T-1$, is a subsequence of $X(T)$ with length 2.

The data set now is the (multi)set of transitions in the sequence $X(T)$, or

$$X = [\langle \xi_{t-1}, \xi_t \rangle | t = 1, \ldots, T-1].$$

The transition $\langle \xi_{t-1}, \xi_t \rangle$ is stored in memory by writing the word ξ_t at ξ_{t-1}. The storing of the data set is illustrated in figure 8.1. This method of storage is just powerful enough to support the prediction (discussed in the preceding subsection) that if A has just happened, B can be expected to happen next.

82   Chapter 8

CONTENTS	ξ_t	ξ_{t+1}	ξ_{t+2}	ξ_{t+3}
ADDRESS	ξ_{t-1}	ξ_t	ξ_{t+1}	ξ_{t+2}

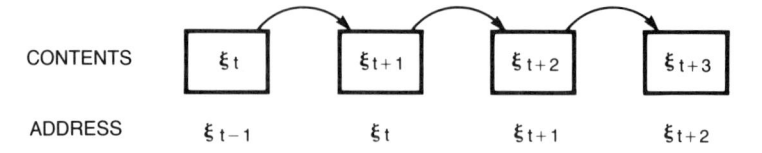

Figure 8.1
Storing transitions in memory.

Convergence to the Stored Sequence

In the best-match problem, a sequence of successively read words was seen either to converge to the best-matching word of the data set or to diverge, depending on the initial distance to the best-matching word. Exactly the same thing cannot happen with stored sequences, but something much like it can.

Let us assume that the memory is loaded well below capacity and that, by and large, the words in $X(T)$ are indifferent to one another. If the memory is now read at ξ_{t-1}, the word ξ_t is retrieved; if it is then read at ξ_t, the word ξ_{t+1} is retrieved; and so forth. So we may write

$$W(\xi_{t-1}) = \xi_t \text{ for } t = 1, \ldots, T-1.$$

If we start by reading at an x that is well within the critical distance of some element ξ_t of the sequence $X(T)$ and if we then read successively, we get the sequence

$$x(0) = x, x(1) = W(x(0)), x(2) = W(x(1)), \ldots.$$

This sequence converges to the stored sequence

$$\xi_t, \xi_{t+1}, \xi_{t+2}, \ldots$$

at the same rate at which the best-match sequence converges to the best-matching word. If the initial distance $d(x, \xi_t)$ is too large, the sequence of $x(i)$'s diverges with respect to the ξ_{t+i}'s—again at the same rate as the best-match sequence does when started equally far from the target. So here the sequence

$$x(0) - \xi_t, x(1) - \xi_{t+1}, x(2) - \xi_{t+2}, \ldots$$

either converges to the zero word or diverges, depending on the initial distance $|x(0) - \xi_t|$. Of course, if that distance is near the critical distance, it may take several iterations before one process or the other takes over. In general, 10 to 20 iterations are enough for the process to either converge or diverge.

For the best-match problem, there is an internal check for deciding whether data or noise words are being read. Reading stored data leads to a converging sequence, which can be detected by seeing whether successively read words approach each other. But when a stored sequence is being retrieved, the read words do not provide such information, because the adjacent words of the original sequence could quite well be orthogonal to one another. Still, there are at least three ways by which to tell whether stored words are being read. Two of them are internal to the memory; one is external.

The first internal criterion is based on the idea that a slight change (1–3 bits) in the initial reading address u will not matter when the series converges (see table 7.2) but will make a great difference when it diverges (see table 7.3). So this criterion is based on the behavior of two sequences that are read by starting from nearly the same address—that is, whether the sequence

$$u - v, W(u) - W(v), W(W(u)) - W(W(v)), \ldots$$

converges to the zero word or diverges when, say, $1 \leq d(u, v) \leq 3$.

The second internal criterion comes from observing the behavior of individual bit sums. The reading of previously stored words is indicated by a large variance in the bit sums; the reading of random noise is indicated by a small variance. This second criterion seems more feasible and attractive physiologically than the first because its engineering problems are simpler and because it applies to all forms of data that can be stored in the memory, not just best-match data and sequences.

The external criterion is interesting because it relates to learning. A stored sequence is an internal representation of the past. The whole idea behind storing it is to have it available when similar events occur in the future. Let us assume that the present moment is $T - 1$, that the past word most similar to the present is ξ_{t-1}, and that we try to predict what is about to happen, namely ξ_T. So we read at ξ_{T-1}. If where we are now (ξ_{T-1}) is sufficiently similar to where we have been before (ξ_{t-1}), we will read the word $W(\xi_{T-1})$, which is very similar to ξ_t. If, in fact, the ongoing experience is similar to the one in the past, the word ξ_t is a good prediction of ξ_T, and therefore the word just retrieved, $W(\xi_{T-1})$, also is. This, then, is the external criterion: How closely do the words read from memory by addressing it with the present situation agree with the unfolding situation? However, if they do not agree, the external criterion provides no clue as to whether previously written words or just random-noise words are being read.

Second- and Higher-Order Prediction: k-fold Prediction

The Best-Match Machine can recognize patterns, but it cannot predict events. Prediction is made possible by storing transitions. Thus far, we have discussed the storing of first-order transitions, and we might call the resulting machines first-order machines (the Best-Match Machine being of order 0). A first-order machine is adequate for predicting events generated by a first-order stochastic process—for example, elements of a Markov chain.

It is easy to demonstrate the need for higher-order prediction. Assume that in $X(T)$ the sequence $\langle A, B, C \rangle$ is usually followed by D, and the sequence $\langle E, B, C \rangle$ by F. To predict the consequences of C, we then need to know what occurred two steps before C. The prediction requires a third-order machine, because to choose between D and F we need to know three preceding terms of the sequence.

In what follows, a special case of higher-order predicting is discussed. It will be called k-fold prediction, and it is particularly well suited for realization in a sparse distributed memory. A k-fold prediction of ξ_T is a composite of k simple predictions of ξ_T that are made from the last k elements, $\xi_{T-k}, \ldots, \xi_{T-1}$. The following vocabulary helps to describe it in detail.

kth-Order Transition A kth-order transition occurring in the sequence $X(T)$ is a subsequence of $X(T)$ of length $k + 1$. For example, $\langle \xi_t, \xi_{t+1}, \xi_{t+2}, \xi_{t+3} \rangle$ is a third-order transition; it says that the three-element sequence $\langle \xi_t, \xi_{t+1}, \xi_{t+2} \rangle$ is followed by ξ_{t+3}.

j-Step Transition A j-step transition is a pair of elements in $X(T)$ separated by $j - 1$ elements. For example, $\langle \xi_t, \xi_{t+3} \rangle$ is a three-step transition; it says that ξ_t, in three steps, is followed by ξ_{t+3}. A first-order transition necessarily is a one-step transition. The reason for considering j-step transitions is that they are easily stored in a random-access memory, as we have already seen with one-step transitions: The first word of the pair is used as the address and the second as the datum (ξ_{t+3} is stored at ξ_t).

j-Step Memory A j-step memory, N'_j, is a (sparse distributed) memory that stores the j-step transitions of $X(T)$. The data retrieved by reading at x will be denoted by $D_j(x)$. It is further assumed that the data become available j time steps *after* the address x has been presented to the memory, so that the memory has a built-in *delay*. Our treatment thus far has been of one-step memories, and there $N' = N'_1$ and $D(x) = D_1(x)$.

k-fold Memory A k-fold memory is a set of k j-step memories, $\{N'_1, \ldots, N'_k\}$. The jth memory, N'_j, is also referred to as the jth fold. Figure 8.2 illustrates the storage of transitions in a threefold memory.

k-fold Data The k-fold data at time T, $D(T)$, are the multiset of data available at time T. From our definitions it follows that

Storage and Retrieval of Sequences   85

WRITING
ADDRESS $\xi 10$ $\xi 11$ $\xi 12$ $\xi 13$ $\xi 14$ $\xi 15$ $\xi 16$

CONTENTS OF LOCATIONS IN THE THREE FOLDS

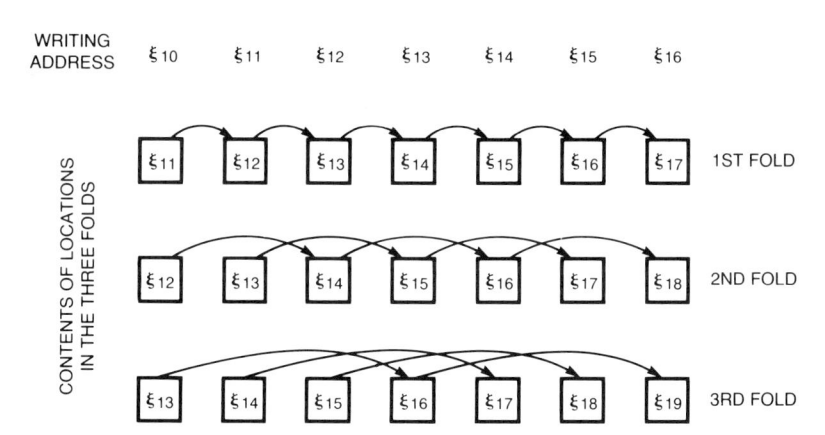

| $\xi 11$ | $\xi 12$ | $\xi 13$ | $\xi 14$ | $\xi 15$ | $\xi 16$ | $\xi 17$ | 1ST FOLD |

| $\xi 12$ | $\xi 13$ | $\xi 14$ | $\xi 15$ | $\xi 16$ | $\xi 17$ | $\xi 18$ | 2ND FOLD |

| $\xi 13$ | $\xi 14$ | $\xi 15$ | $\xi 16$ | $\xi 17$ | $\xi 18$ | $\xi 19$ | 3RD FOLD |

Figure 8.2
Transitions of a threefold memory.

$$D(T) = \biguplus_{j=1,\ldots,k} D_j(\xi_{T-j}).$$

These data combine information from the transitions, up to the length of k steps, that are pertinent to the prediction of ξ_T. If we assume that the access radius is the same in all folds, the *weight* of the data from the jth fold—that is, the weight of the prediction from j steps back—is proportional to the number of locations in the jth fold, N_j'.

The word read at time T, $W(T)$, is a representative of the pooled data, $D(T)$. How this representative can be computed from such data has been discussed at length in chapter 7.

k-fold Prediction   Finally, a k-fold prediction of ξ_T is the word read at time T, $W(T)$. To summarize somewhat inaccurately: ξ_t, the state at moment t, provides an independent prediction for each of the moments $t + 1, \ldots, t + k$, and hence each of the states $\xi_{T-k}, \ldots, \xi_{T-1}$ provides an independent prediction of ξ_T, all of which are then combined to form a single prediction of ξ_T. Reading at ξ_{T-1} to predict ξ_T with $W(\xi_{T-1})$ is an example of a onefold prediction.

To illustrate the idea further, let us derive a threefold prediction from data in which the third-order transitions $\langle A, B, C, D \rangle$ and $\langle E, B, C, F \rangle$ are equally probable. The task is to predict either D or F on the basis of whether $\langle A, B, C \rangle$ or $\langle E, B, C \rangle$ has just happened. Assume that the transitions are stored in three equally probable folds, that is, that $N_1' = N_2' = N_3'$. The third-order transitions $\langle A, B, C, D \rangle$ and $\langle E, B, C, F \rangle$ give rise to the multiset $[\langle A, D \rangle, \langle E, F \rangle]$ of three-step transitions, the multiset $[\langle A, C \rangle, \langle B, D \rangle, \langle E, C \rangle, \langle B, F \rangle]$ of two-step transitions, and the multiset $[\langle A, B \rangle,$

⟨B, C⟩, ⟨C, D⟩, ⟨E, B⟩, ⟨B, C⟩, ⟨C, F⟩] of one-step transitions. After ⟨A, B, C⟩ has just happened, the pooled data will contain one D from the three-step transition ⟨A, D⟩, one D and one F from the two-step transitions ⟨B, D⟩ and ⟨B, F⟩, respectively, and one D and one F from the one-step transitions ⟨C, D⟩ and ⟨C, F⟩, respectively, for a total of three D's and two F's. The prediction will then be D. Similarly, after ⟨E, B, C⟩ the data will be [D, D, F, F, F] and the prediction will be F.

As was already mentioned, this brief discussion of higher-order predictions was included because of the limited usefulness of first-order predictions in real-life situations. The k-fold predictions recommend themselves by being easy to realize, as will be seen in the next chapter.

Interpretations

Recalling or recognizing a learned sequence—the alphabet, speech patterns, telephone numbers, poetry, music—lends support to the notion that a retrieval cue retrieves its consequences with delays that correspond to the delays when the sequence was stored. According to the theory, the kth fold of the memory stores simple transitions that span k time steps (by writing ξ_t at ξ_{t-k}). Available from memory at time T are, then, the k-step predictions based on ξ_{T-k} ($k = 1, 2, 3, \ldots$), or, rather, what is gotten by pooling those predictions. When a learned sequence is recalled, the predictions reinforce one another, increasing the probability of the recall of the next item in the sequence.

Further support for the presence of the delays is provided by the following two observations: First, if we fail to recall the next item at some point in a sequence, a good strategy is to take a new running start—that is, to back up a little (say, 3–6 items) and start recalling from there on. That seems to improve the recall of the temporarily lost item. The explanation offered by the model is that many preceding items are made to contribute maximally toward the recall of the next item, whereas trying to recall it from the present item alone brings only its contribution into play. Second, rhythm is more important than tempo in recognizing a tune, assuming correct pitch. Changing the time scale within fairly wide limits (speeding a piece up or slowing it down) presents no major difficulty (the nervous system adjusts to it easily), but changing the relative durations of the notes at random is very confusing. The model predicts this behavior if we allow in it one parameter that adjusts the time scale of all folds equally.

Chapter 9
Constructing Distributed Memory

Thus far I have developed a theory of memory and have provided a mathematical model of it: a sparse random-access memory in which an item is stored by distributing copies of it in many storage locations. In doing so, I have made frequent reference to the neuron, emphasizing its suitability for address decoding and also for storing information. This chapter is concerned with the construction of a physical memory from neuronlike components and with the comparison of real structures found in the brain with the constructed memory.

The memory that will be constructed can be characterized as follows:

Addressing The memory will be built of addressable storage locations. A location is activated whenever a read or write address is within a certain number of bits of the location's address.

Storage For storing information, a storage location has n counters, one for each bit position.

Writing Information is stored by incrementing a counter to store a bit that is 1 (and possibly decrementing a counter to store a bit that is 0—more will be said about this later).

Reading Information is retrieved by pooling the contents of the storage locations activated by the read address and then finding, for each bit, whether zeros or ones are in the majority.

Let us start with address decoding. A storage location should be accessible from anywhere within r_p bits of the location's address. That means that (linear-threshold) neurons can be used for address decoding. The threshold of each address-decoder neuron would be set *permanently* to r_p units below the neuron's maximum weighted sum.

There are two other ways of working with the thresholds, both of which seem physiologically feasible and have been discussed above. First, the access region could be found dynamically for each location by adjusting the threshold of the address-decoder neuron to the level where the neuron fires with an average frequency of p. Second, the adjusting of thresholds could be used as a mechanism for searching memory. These two ways will not be explored further in this book.

88   Chapter 9

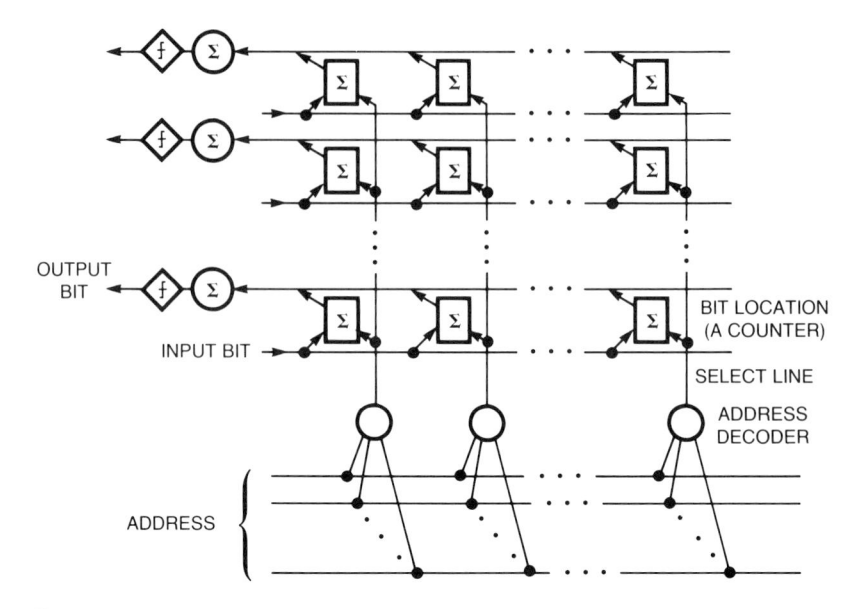

Figure 9.1
Three storage locations of a sparse distributed memory.

Reading at x is done by pooling the contents of the locations accessible from x and finding the average word $W(x)$. The average can be computed from n bitwise sums, and hence a storage location (one associated with an address decoder—a hard location) can be realized as n counters, the ith one counting bits in the ith position. In computing the average word, the pooled bit sums are compared with a threshold. The mean bit sum over all the data stored in memory can be used for the threshold. Figure 9.1 shows three storage locations of a memory that can work in this way. Notice the likeness of these locations to the locations of a computer memory (figure 2.3).

Other roughly equivalent counting schemes could be used, and some might agree better with the properties of real neurons than does the one presented here. Recall that a neuron adds weighted inputs. If the synaptic weights of a neuron could be changed selectively by other neurons, the synapses could serve as the bit counters. However, since the sign of a synaptic weight cannot change, the counters could not work exactly as outlined above. Instead, they could count just the 1 bits, and the pooled count could then be compared with the mean count of ones to decide whether a bit of a read word is 1. In constructing the physical model, we shall assume that the contents of memory locations are stored in adjustable synapses.

Since computing the average vector calls for an individual counter for each bit of a location, a word location is broken into *bit locations*. That means that a storage location—one associated with a single address-decoder neuron—need not have all n counters. The ultimate distributed sparse memory would have an individual address decoder for each bit location, although that would waste address decoders. Thus, in our construction of the physical model we assume that the synapses along the axon of an address-decoder neuron serve as bit locations, that each axon makes synapses with many neurons of another class, and that those neurons provide the output from memory. The pooling of the bit sums and the computing of the average is a linear threshold function that seems suitable for realizing with neurons.

This construction applies for a memory for first-order prediction, that is, a single fold. To construct a kth-order predictor involves constructing k first-order predictors with delays $1, \ldots, k$ and pooling the predictions to a single prediction. Such a k-fold memory requires that a delay be associated with each storage location. The function of the delay is to activate the location a fixed number of time steps *after* an address that selects the location has been presented to the memory. The delay could be achieved by delaying address-decoder input or address-decoder output. Apart from the delays the folds are identical, and the pooling of the data over many folds is like pooling it over a single fold, meaning that a multifold memory looks just like a single-fold memory. The probabilities of the folds are included in the design automatically; they are proportional to the numbers of storage locations with different delays.

Notice an interesting thing about the delays: The storage locations do not "care" what the delays are, only that they are the same in storing and in retrieving the data. This suggests an even more general memory: It really does not matter how an address-decoder output is generated so long as it is regenerated under the same or similar conditions, for then the data will be retrieved whenever the conditions are similar to those under which they were stored. In other words, what matters is that the decoding of an address be repeatable; that is what ultimately allows an organ to serve the function of memory. The firing of an address decoder simply represents some particular condition or kind of activity in the system's (most recent) past, and the recurrence of that condition brings about storage in and retrieval from particular locations. So it is even possible that the firing of an address-decoder neuron signals that some specific *sequence* of events has just occurred. Of course, the address space and the datum space would then be different; however, the transmission lines for storing and retrieving the data would still have to come in matched pairs, and this leads to the next topic.

An Important Detail of Architecture

We will now take a close look at constructing a bit location. A bit location should have three lines or connections: one coming to it from an address decoder for selecting the location, one leading away from it to allow its contents to be read, and—this is important—one leading to it to allow its contents to be updated. Activity on the address-decoder line activates the location for a read or write operation, but it alone cannot effect the writing into the location. For that, we need the data-input lines.

It is important to understand the relation between the data-input line and the data-output line of a bit location: One brings in the data that the other will retrieve at some later time. The implications of this seemingly innocent observation are significant. Since many bit locations are pooled to form a single bit of output from memory, they must be connected to a common output line. Storing the data, then, calls for a matching network that takes one input line and distributes it to the very bit locations that are pooled for a single bit of output. In computer memories, the same wire can be used for both input and output; however, since neurons conduct in one direction only, neuron memories must have separate input and output lines. What is significant is that input and output lines should correspond to one another, one for one, and therefore they should run in matched pairs.

This architectural detail—*matched pairs of input and output lines*—can help us find potential storage locations in the nervous system. The presence of such pairs in the cerebellum has led me to speculate that the cerebellum is a random-access memory of the kind described here. This is the topic of the next section.

Cerebellar Cortex as a Random-Access Memory

The usefulness of a theory is measured by its ability to explain observations, to simplify old explanations, to predict, and to inspire discovery. A theory can be beneficial without even being correct, for it can stimulate the discovery of a better theory. In attempting to refute or disprove it we can notice things that have been previously overlooked. But it is important that a theory make a claim the validity of which can be verified or refuted.

In proposing this theory as relevant to memory in the brain, I should indicate where in the brain such a memory might be found. The architecture of the cerebellar cortex is most suggestive, although the theory does not ascribe functions to all its cells or to all its connections. The relation of input and output to the cortex, however, is an important part of the interpretation. This interpretation is the third major result of the present study.

Gross Anatomy of Cerebellar Cortex The cerebellum is a well-differentiated part of the brain located behind and below the cerebral hemispheres (in humans). Its design is highly regular and quite uniform over a large number of animal species. Its functions are to coordinate movements and to maintain the body's physical equilibrium.

The cerebellum has been the object of detailed study since the latter part of the nineteenth century. A concise description of its anatomy and physiology has been given by Llinás (1975). For details, see Eccles et al. 1967 and Palay and Chan-Palay 1974. A summary of Eccles et al. has been given by Marr (1969).

The principal cell types of the cerebellar cortex are excitatory granule cells, inhibitory Purkinje cells, inhibitory basket cells, inhibitory stellate cells, and inhibitory Golgi cells. Input to the cerebellar cortex is by mossy fibers and climbing fibers, both of which are excitatory. The Purkinje cells provide the sole output of the cortex. Figure 9.2 shows the neurons of the cerebellar cortex.

The cortex is organized in two layers: the inner or *granular* layer and the outer or *molecular* layer. The cell bodies of the Purkinje cells define the border between the two. The Purkinje-cell dendrites are in the outer layer, and the axons leave the cortex through the inner layer.

The *granule cells* occupy the inner layer. They are relatively simple and are abundant. Over half of the neurons in the nervous system (possibly as many as 10^{11}) are granule cells of the cerebellum. A granule cell has 3–5 dendrites, and the cell's axon rises to the outer layer, where it divides into two branches in the shape of the letter T. The tops of the T's form the *parallel fibers*, which synapse with the other four cell types of the cerebellar cortex.

The granule cells receive input from the *mossy fibers* (which are axons of neurons outside the cerebellar cortex) and from the Golgi cells. A single mossy fiber forms synapses with a great number of granule cells. Of all axons of the nervous system, a mossy fiber forms synapses with the greatest number of neurons.

The *Purkinje cells* are aligned, almost in rows, perpendicular to the parallel fibers. The broad and flat dendrite systems of a row form a plane perpendicular to the parallel fibers. The dendrite planes are stacked side by side like books on a shelf, and a single parallel fiber passes through many (200–450) such planes, forming synapses in some if not all of them (estimates range from 45 to 450). The arrangement is ideal for bringing many parallel fibers into contact with many Purkinje cells. The dendrite system of one Purkinje cell intersects as many as 400,000 parallel fibers and forms synapses with some or all of them. No other neuron in the nervous system receives input from as many neurons. Other inputs to the Purkinje cells come from the stellate cells, the basket cells, and the climbing fibers.

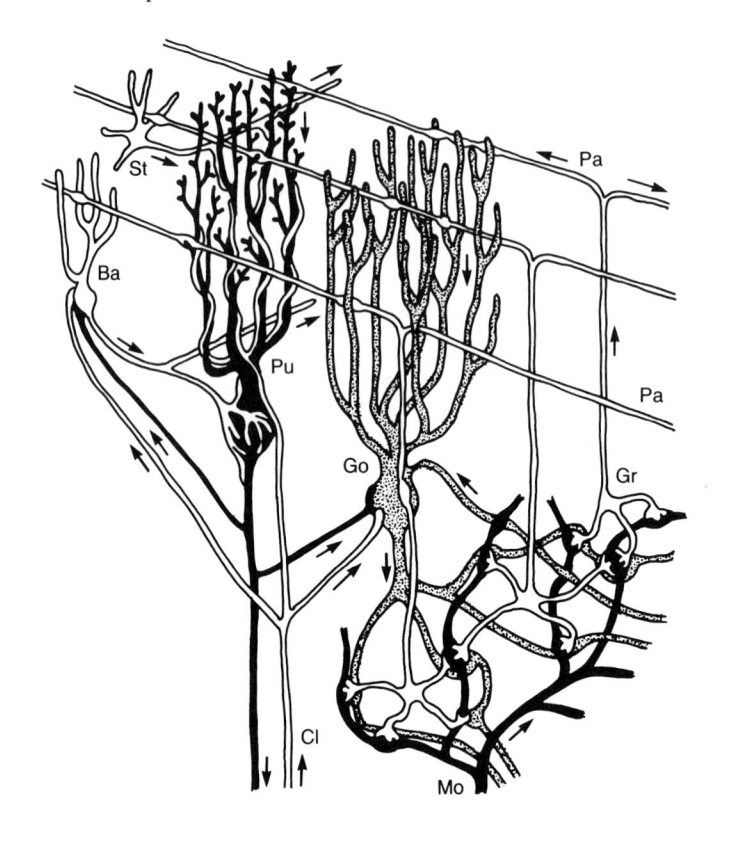

Pu = Purkinje cell (black)
Go = Golgi cell (dotted)
Gr = granule cell
Pa = parallel fiber

St = stellate cell
Ba = basket cell
Cl = climbing fiber
Mo = mossy fiber (black)

Figure 9.2
Neurons of the cerebellar cortex. (Source: Llinás 1975. Copyright © 1975 by Scientific American, Inc. All rights reserved.)

Besides leaving the cortex, branches of the Purkinje-cell axon go to basket cells and Golgi cells.

Stellate and *basket cells* reside in the outer layer. A cell of either kind receives input from the parallel fibers, and its output goes, by way of inhibitory synapses, to a row of Purkinje cells. The basket cells also receive input from the climbing fibers and the Purkinje cells.

Golgi-cell input is about as varied as Purkinje-cell input; it comes mostly from the parallel fibers but also from the mossy fibers, the climbing fibers, and the Purkinje cells. Golgi-cell output goes to the granule cells. Golgi-cell axons and mossy fibers form special double synapses with the dendrites of the granule cells.

The *climbing fibers* pair off, one for one, with the Purkinje cells. A climbing fiber follows the dendrites of its Purkinje cell, branching where they branch (hence the name), and forms many synapses with the dendrites. The firing of a climbing fiber guarantees the firing of the Purkinje cell. Climbing fibers provide input also to basket cells and Golgi cells.

Interpretation The parts of the cerebellar circuit that I interpret here are the mossy fibers, the granule cells (with their parallel fibers), the stellate cells, the basket cells, the Purkinje cells, and the climbing fibers. The interpretation is based on the architecture of this circuit; it seems well suited for realizing a random-access memory (a fact that I noticed only after developing the theory). The fit is by no means perfect, but parts of it are so compelling that they deserve comment.

The mossy fibers would be the address lines. They come from outside the cerebellar cortex, and they form synapses with a great many granule cells. The granule cells—their dendrites and bodies—would be the address decoders, marking the hard locations N'. The granule cells are the most numerous of all neurons—which is fitting, since each storage location needs a neuron for an address decoder. According to estimates of the number of granule cells, the cerebellum could have as many as 10^{11} storage locations.

The bit locations would then be somewhere along the granule-cell axons—that is, along the parallel fibers. The synapses of the parallel fibers with the Purkinje cells would be the bit locations, and the function of a Purkinje cell would be to pool, or to sum up, the contents of bit locations of many different storage locations to a single bit of output from memory. The stellate and basket cells could adjust the thresholds of the Purkinje cells to decide whether zeros or ones are more frequent in the pooled data. Finally, the climbing fibers would be the data-input lines, for they pair with the outputs (with the Purkinje cells) and they go to the vicinity of the bit locations. This coincidence of the climbing fibers with the dendrites of the Purkinje cells—of input lines with output lines—is what first drew my

94   Chapter 9

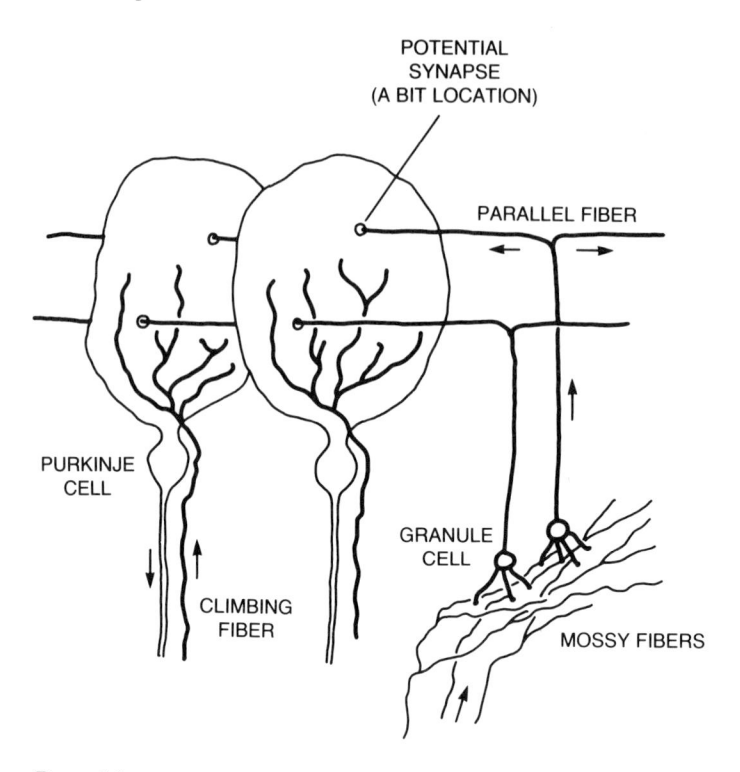

Figure 9.3
Part of the cerebellar circuit.

attention to the cerebellar cortex. Figure 9.2 is a reproduction of the picture in which I had seen this pairing of neurons. The main circuit involved with the proposed memory function is shown in figure 9.3.

In a comparison with the random-access (core) memory of a conventional computer, a parallel fiber corresponds to the wire that passes through the cores of a memory location, the (potential) synapses with the Purkinje cells correspond to the bit slots of a memory register, and the flat dendrite tree of a Purkinje cell corresponds to a bit plane. A parallel fiber that passes through 400 dendrite planes would stand for a 400-bit location.

According to this interpretation, the weights of the Purkinje-cell synapses with the parallel fibers represent the stored data. Whether the synaptic weights are actually affected by input from the climbing fibers is, at least for me, speculation. However, the response of a Purkinje cell to an input along a climbing fiber is so predictable and strong that it could serve some specific purpose, such as the updating of memory. If each potential synapse were to represent just one bit of information, the capacity of the human cerebellum memory would be somewhere around 4×10^{13} bits.

The absence of inhibitory input from the outside to the cerebellar cortex and the very small numbers of dendrites of the granule cells and of input synapses made by them (3–5 inputs per granule cell) raise a question about address decoding. According to the theory, most address-decoder neurons should have about the same number—$n/2$ each—of excitatory and inhibitory inputs. This is clearly not the case with the granule cells. However, the granule cells could possibly carry out the final stage of address decoding, the earlier stages of which are performed outside the cerebellum.

If one looks only at the architecture of the memory and not at that of the circuits that make use of the memory, one can tell only whether the memory is a random-access memory in the sense discussed here. The architecture of the cerebellar cortex is that of a random-access memory. This study leaves open the issue of whether addresses to the memory are used as data in the cerebellum.

Chapter 10
The Organization of an Autonomous Learning System

This final chapter is about systems that function independently, that interact with their environments and record their interactions, and that therefore have the potential for learning and adaptation. How do such systems work?

In trying to answer this question, we are guided by examples from nature. We can look at animals and ask what kind of internal organization sustains their autonomous, adaptive behavior. Because of the subject matter of this book, the quest has a special emphasis: If the system has a sparse distributed memory for recording its past, what besides the memory does it need, and what is the overall organization of the system like?

Memory for Patterns and Pattern Sequences

Let us first review the memory and see what functions it can sustain. Then the other necessary functions must be accomplished by other parts of the system.

The sparse distributed memory, as described in this book, works with long vectors of bits. These vectors can be thought of as patterns of binary features. The mathematics generalizes readily to patterns of multivalued features, the most important thing being that the number of features be large. From here on we assume that the features need not be binary. What we have, then, is a memory that can be addressed by large patterns of multivalued features and that can store these very same patterns.

Because a pattern can be used both as an address and as a datum, a sequence of patterns can be stored as a pointer chain. The first pattern in the sequence is used as the address in storing the second pattern, the second as the address in storing the third, and so forth. Any pattern in the sequence can then serve as a retrieval cue that will initiate the retrieval of the rest of the sequence.

Addressing the memory need not be exact. A previously stored pattern can be retrieved not only with the pattern's original storage address but also with addresses similar to it. In general, the address patterns that have been used as write addresses attract, meaning that reading within the critical distance of such an address retrieves a pattern that is closer to the written pattern, on the average, than the read address is to the write address.

This attractor property is fundamental to pattern recognition and sequence recall. To use the memory for recognizing a set of patterns, each pattern is stored with the pattern itself as the address; to use it for recalling sequences of patterns, each sequence is stored as a pointer chain. Reading from the memory is the same in either case: The pattern just read is used as the next read address. Since write addresses attract, the initial read address need not be exact. If it is well within the critical distance of some previous write address, 3–6 iterations will usually suffice to read patterns exactly as written. In other words, successive reading brings us closer and closer to, and actually finds, a stored pattern or sequence.

The memory groups patterns automatically, providing for two kinds of generalization or abstraction. One kind is the attraction by stored patterns and sequences: To read from the memory, we need not know the exact address patterns that were used in writing into the memory. The other kind is when many similar patterns have been used as write addresses. Then the individual patterns written with those addresses cannot be recovered exactly. What is recovered, instead, is a statistical average of the patterns written in that neighborhood of addresses. This generalization is in terms of the features that make up the patterns. The features that are common to all or most of the patterns in the neighborhood will stand out as an encoding for a cluster of patterns.

For example, the memory might be used for recognizing visual patterns. An object viewed from slightly different angles and distances will then produce a set of similar patterns. This being a pattern-recognition task, each pattern is stored with itself as the address. Consequently, many similar addresses will be used in writing into the memory, and they will select many common locations. Reading at any of these write addresses or at nearby addresses is then unlikely to yield a stored pattern exactly. Instead, the memory will produce patterns representing the object in an abstract sense rather than patterns representing any specific views of it. Some features of these aggregate patterns will be prominent; others will be unimportant. Mathematically, the object occupies a region of the pattern space with poorly defined boundaries.

The predictive power of the memory is based on its ability to retrieve sequences and to generalize. If a system's past is represented as a sequence of patterns and if this sequence has been stored in memory, the pattern representing the present moment can be used as an address to retrieve the consequences of similar moments in the past.

Modeling the World

As we—intelligent beings in general—interact with the world, we become better and better at dealing with the world. We say that we learn from experience. Our experiences are stored so that we can predict what is likely to happen and to choose appropriate action, for example, to avoid danger or to seek reward. Many things appear to be learned by nothing more than repeated exposure to them.

We can think of learning as model building. We build an internal model of the world and then operate with the model. What can we say about this model on the basis of how we behave and how our behavior changes with experience?

1. The modeling is so basic to our nature that we are hardly aware of it. It might even be said that this modeling is our way of understanding the world. We understand what is happening only to the extent that we are able to predict what is going to happen, and the internal model is our means of predicting. Again, we are mostly unaware that any predicting is even going on; we just do it because of the way we are built.

2. The modeling mechanism constructs objects and individuals. A person, a tree, a river are constantly changing, and our views of them are different at different times, yet we perceive them as "that person," or "that tree" (or "that species of tree"), or "that river."

3. Operating with the model is a little like operating with a scale model. Not only does the model have individuals and objects; it also mimics their actions and interactions. The more experience we have had, the more faithfully are the dynamics of the world reproduced by the model. This manifests itself in our habitual formation of expectations. For example, having experienced lightning followed by thunder many times, we come to expect thunder whenever we see a bright flash of lightning. Psychological experiments on classical (Pavlovian) conditioning show that proper juxtaposition in time is all that is needed for such expectations to form. The model simply captures statistical regularities of the world, as mediated by the senses, and is able to reproduce them later.

4. Our world model includes ourselves as a part. For example, we can prepare ourselves for a situation by imagining ourselves in the situation. When we do that, we get an idea of how we are likely to feel or act in the situation.

5. There is oneness to our subjective experience, whether that experience is dominated by the outside world or by our internal model of it. In normal, day-by-day life we are constantly in touch with the outside world through our senses. For us, the world is the way our senses report it to be. When we build our internal model of the world, the report of the senses is

all that we have to go by. If the recording is faithful, the model can recreate a subjective experience that has been created by the world.

Ordinarily there is sufficient difference between the quality of the experience produced by the world (as mediated by the senses) and that produced by the internal model to let us keep the two apart. For example, we are quite confident that there is water in the pool when we look down from a diving board and see water. On the other hand, even if we can imagine ourselves flying by merely spreading our arms, we are not likely to jump off a cliff. Thus, we tend to recognize some experiences as real and others as imagined. This, however, is not always the case, as dreams and hallucinations illustrate. They are produced almost entirely by the internal model, but to us they can be very real, capable of producing physical signs of pleasure or fear, for example. In extreme cases we may be unable to tell whether the thing actually happened or whether we just "made it up." The point here is that the (subjective) experience produced by the world is of the same quality as that produced by the internal model of the world; there is no fundamental difference between the two from the subject's point of view.

6. Our internal and external "pictures" merge without our being aware of it. We scan our surroundings for overall cues and fill in much of the detail from the internal model. However, when something unusual happens, we begin to pay attention. We are alerted by the discrepancy between the external report of what is happening and the internal report of what should be happening on the basis of past experience.

Driving along a thoroughly familiar road is a good example. We know its turns and intersections so well that we hardly pay attention to details that usually stay unchanged; we rely on the internal model for such details. When some detail changes, as when a new stop sign appears overnight, it is the regular travelers who are the more likely ones to run it on their first few trips past the spot. They usually become aware of the new sign just after running it, and they experience startle.

7. The internal model affects our perception profoundly, again without our being aware of it. This is demonstrated by eyewitness accounts of crimes and accidents, particularly when the witness is prejudiced toward one of the parties involved (Loftus 1979). The *pre*judgments are the product of the internal model. In general, perception involves the relating of the present sensory input to past input, which requires memory.

Storing the World Model in Sparse Distributed Memory

If intelligent behavior is based on modeling, what are the modeling mechanisms? I will postulate that memory stores and maintains the model and allows its use. Therefore, the memory must store a record of the system's past in a way that allows the system to predict what is about to happen, to plan action, and to act according to a plan.

For the purposes of the following discussion, let us say that at any given moment the individual is in some subjective mental state. A flow of these states, represented here by a sequence of states, then describes the individual's (subjective) experience over time. The world itself can likewise be described by a sequence of states, but the state space for the world is immense in comparison with that for an individual's experience.

I have emphasized above that a person's experience is influenced strongly by the world as reported by the senses, and that it can be influenced equally by the internal model—by what is retrieved from memory. The simplest way to build the world model, then, is to store the report of the senses in memory and to retrieve it later from there. If it is retrieved faithfully and allowed to feed into the subjective experience in the same way as the senses feed into it, there is no way for the individual to distinguish an experience created by the internal model from one created by the outside world.

To store the world model in a sparse distributed memory, we need to represent an individual's sensory information at a moment as a long vector of features and let a sequence of such vectors represent the passage of time. The memory works well with such sequences, and above all else it stores and recalls them naturally.

We can now begin to look at the overall organization of a system that models the world and that maintains the model in a sparse distributed memory. Since information supplied by the senses and information supplied by the memory can produce the same subjective experience, it is reasonable to assume that some common part of the architecture is responsible for the system's subjective experience about the world, and that both the senses and the memory feed into it. I will call this part of the architecture the system's *focus*. The system's *subjective experience* about the world over time is then represented by a *sequence of patterns in the focus*. By storing this sequence in memory, the memory can later recreate it in the focus. Figure 10.1 shows the relation of the senses and the memory to the focus.

Because sequences are stored as pointer chains, the patterns of a sequence are used both as addresses and as data. In computer terms, the focus is a combined address-datum register, meaning that the memory is addressed by the focus, the contents of the focus are written into the memory, and the data from the memory feed into the focus. Thus, when the present resembles the past, the senses create a sequence in the focus that resembles a stored sequence. When this sensory sequence is used to address the memory, the memory responds with what the consequences have been in the past. Comparing those past consequences against what happens this time gives the system a criterion for updating its world model.

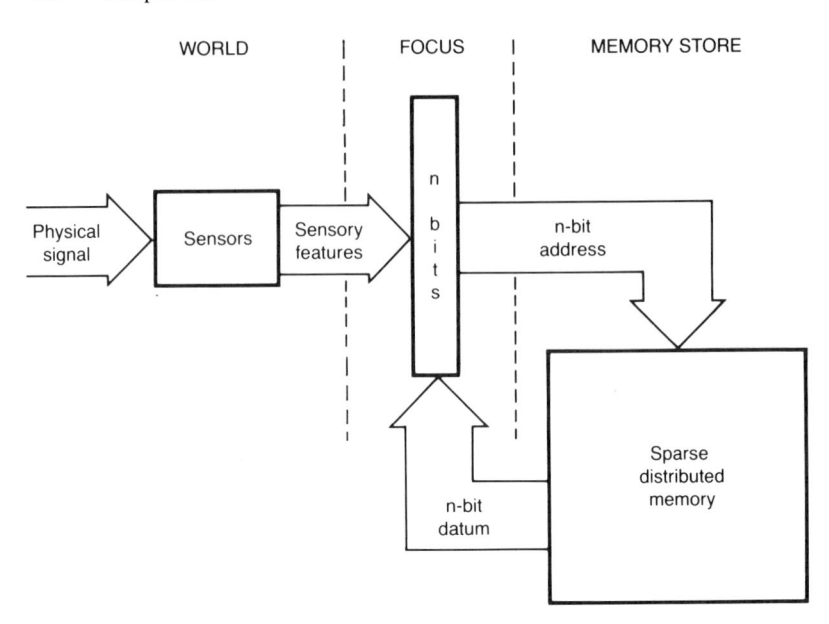

Figure 10.1
Senses, memory, and focus.

The world model is updated by writing into the memory as follows. The pattern held in the focus at time t is used to address the memory, activating a set of memory locations. The response read from those locations is the memory's prediction of the sensory input at time $t + 1$. If the prediction agrees with the sensory input, there is no need to adjust the memory; the read pattern simply becomes the contents of the focus at time $t + 1$. If the two disagree, however, a third, "correct" pattern is computed from them, and it becomes the contents of the focus at time $t + 1$; however, before it is used to address the memory (at time $t + 1$), it is written in the locations from which the "erroneous" output was just read (i.e., in the locations selected at time t). In the simplest case, this third (correct) pattern is just the sensory input at time $t + 1$.

In a more sophisticated updating of the world model, the memory is modified by writing error-correction patterns into it. The corrections for individual pattern components are based on the sum pattern in addition to the final, thresholded output pattern. If the output pattern is in error, the sum pattern can be used to find out by how much each bit counter in the selected locations has to be corrected for the final output to be right. The components of the correction pattern will then not be binary but will range over a larger set of values. As the correction patterns are written in memory over time, the memory builds a better and better model of the world, constrained only by the senses' ability to discriminate and the memory's capacity to store information.

Including Action in the World Model

So far we have seen how an autonomous learning system (an individual) can build an internal model of the world from the report of the senses. Besides observing the world and learning about it, the system also acts and learns from its interaction with the world. To act, the system needs motors (effectors); to learn, it must model its own actions.

The above discussion of a system's internal model of the world postulated the need for something like the focus and that the system's private, subjective experience is based on the contents of the focus. In trying to decide how to include the system's actions in its world model, let us start with the most public aspect of the system's operation: its observable actions.

The observable actions of humans and animals result from the contraction and relaxation of selected muscles. The muscles are controlled by neural signals that originate mostly in the brain, where the signals can be regarded as sequences of patterns over time, akin to the sensory signals. Learning to perform actions then means learning to reproduce sequences of patterns that drive the muscles. This suggests that the system's own actions can be included in the world model by storing motor sequences in memory in addition to sensory sequences. Since the way in and out of the memory is through the focus, the system's motors should be driven from the focus, and since the system's subjective experience is based on the information in the focus, deliberate action becomes part of the system's subjective experience without the need for additional mechanisms. This is fundamentally important to my theory of autonomous learning systems.

The organization of such a system is shown in figure 10.2. A simple, idealized way to think about it is to assume that some components of the focus (well over 50 percent of them) correspond to and can be controlled by the system's sensors, and others (say, 10–20 percent) drive the system's motors, in addition to which the focus could have components with no immediate external significance. Naturally, all components of the focus can also be controlled by the memory. Retrieving well-behaved sequences from the memory to the motor part of the focus would then cause the corresponding actions to be executed by the system.

This organization makes it easy to describe simple forms of cued behavior. Let us assume that the stimulus sequence $\langle A, B, C \rangle$ is to elicit the response sequence $\langle X, Y, Z \rangle$, with A triggering X after one time step and with the two sequences running in lockstep from then on. The pattern

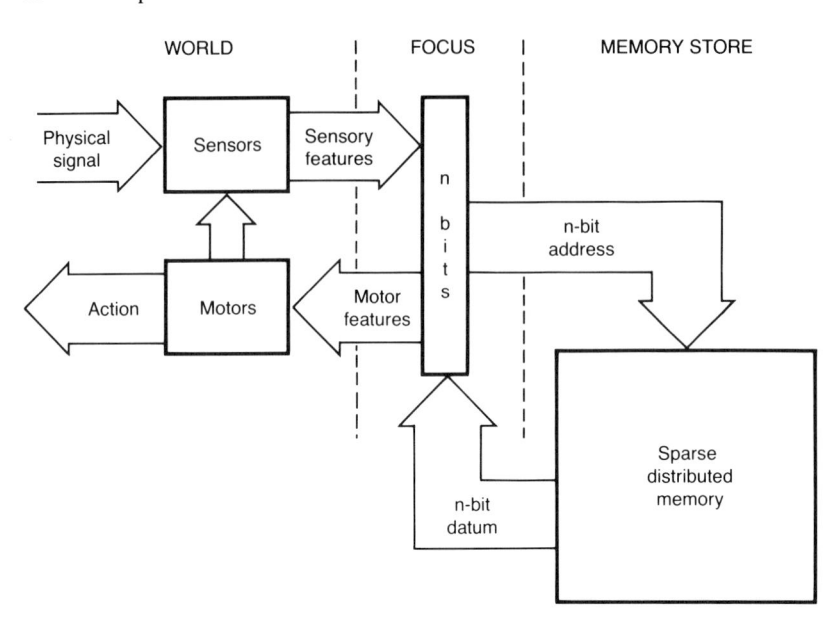

Figure 10.2
Organization of an autonomous system.

sequence that needs to be generated in the focus can then be written as $\langle Aw, BX, CY, dZ \rangle$, where the first letter in each pair corresponds to the sensory-input section and the second to the motor-output section of the focus, and where the lower-case letters w and d stand for parts of patterns unspecified by the problem statement. A sensory input can be thought of as occupying 80 percent of the components of the focus, and a motor output as occupying the remaining 20 percent. Assume that the sequence $\langle AW, BX, CY, DZ \rangle$ has been written in memory (the previously unspecified w and d have specific values W and D in the sequence that has been stored), and that A is present (that is, presented to the focus through the senses). Then Aw, which is similar to AW, will be used as an address, and therefore BX is likely to be retrieved from the memory into the focus. This means that the action caused by X (action X, for short) will be performed at the time at which B is expected to be observed. If the sensory report agrees with B, then BX will be used as the next memory address and CY will be retrieved, causing the action Y. If at that time the report of the senses agrees with C, then CY will be used to read DZ, which completes the execution of the action sequence $\langle X, Y, Z \rangle$.

This example raises several questions: (1) Will the sequence be recalled and the actions performed every time the stimulus A is present? (2) Will the action sequence always be completed once it has started? (3) How might a system be trained for the sequence? The mathematical properties of the memory provide the following answers:

1. If stimulus A controls more than 80 percent of the focus (the critical distance in the examples of chapter 7 is 209 bits out of 1,000), then presenting A will initiate a sequence of reads that tracks the stored sequence, no matter what the unspecified part w of the initial pattern Aw is. However, if A controls significantly less than 80 percent of the focus, or if the cue is not exactly A but a similar pattern A', then Aw or $A'w$ may not be sufficiently close to the original write address AW to cause BX (or something close to BX) to be retrieved. To read BX, it is then important that the action part w be similar to W.

By equating intentions and subjective states of receptiveness with actions, we come to a rather interesting interpretation of the above: Sometimes a system will respond properly to a cue only if it is waiting for the cue. For an example, assume that the action W means that the system is paying attention and is waiting for a cue, and that w means that the system is performing some other action. If A or A' is then presented, the memory will be addressed with AW or $A'W$, and BX will be retrieved (see the preceding paragraph), whereas Aw or $A'w$ could be too far from AW to cause BX to be retrieved. This means that the system's response to a cue depends on its state at the time the cue is presented. Other cues may be needed to get it in that desired, receptive state. The state might be described as the system's willingness to cooperate.

2. The second question concerns the completion of an action sequence. In terms of our example, the sequence $\langle AW, BX, CY, DZ \rangle$ has been written in memory, and BX has been read successfully from memory. If input from the senses is now suppressed, the focus will be controlled entirely by the memory, and the rest of the sequence will be recalled and the action completed.

Let us assume, however, that the senses are not blocked off, and that they feed the sequence $\langle A, B, K, L \rangle$ into the focus instead of the expected $\langle A, B, C, D \rangle$, where K and L are quite different from C and D. Then BX will retrieve CY, meaning that Y is executed and C is expected to be sensed. But since the senses report K, the next contents of the focus will be not CY but HY (where H is some combination of C and K that, in general, is quite different from C). Consequently, HY is too far from CY for anything like DZ to be retrieved, and this causes the last action, Z, to fail.

This failure can be interpreted in several ways. The simplest is to think of the system as monitoring its environment and ceasing to act when the proper cues are no longer present. We might say then that the response is driven by the stimulus, or that the action is maintained by the environment. The interesting thing is that the action can affect the environment. We can think of the system as monitoring the effects of its own actions, and that when the *effects* no longer confirm the system's expectations (e.g., when K is observed when C is expected) the action stops, whereas the system could have completed it—however inappropriately—had it not been monitoring its environment.

This example demonstrates how the system's own actions and their effects can be a part of the system's internal model of the world. As the system acts and since the action is a part of the pattern that addresses the memory, the pattern retrieved from the memory includes an expectation of the action's results—that is, what usually happened on previous occasions right after the action was performed. The world model, or memory, can then be used not only to monitor the course of actions but also to plan action. To plan, the system must initiate the "thought" in the focus and then block off the present (that is, ignore environmental cues and suppress the execution of actions). The memory will then retrieve into the focus the likely consequences of the contemplated actions.

In this section the use of the words 'stimulus' and 'response' may seem strange to someone accustomed to the literature of psychology, where they are defined from a point of view external to an organism, the stimulus being presented to the sensory system and the response being mediated by the motor system. From the point of view of the memory, however, the entire pattern in the focus, including both sensory (stimulus) and motor (response) components, is one big stimulus, and the memory responds with a pattern that likewise contains both sensory and motor components.

3. The third question is about the learning of sequences of actions, which is essential if a system is to be adaptive. It is discussed in the following section.

Learning to Act

A system's model of the world is built from sequences of patterns in the focus, and the model's goodness is judged by how well it predicts such sequences. When the model predicts incorrectly, it is adjusted.

Regarding sensory experience, the world feeds correct sequences into the focus through the senses, so that the world decides whether a sensory prediction coming from memory is correct. If it is not (that is, if the memory's prediction disagrees with the report of the senses), then the memory is adjusted toward the report of the senses.

Regarding action, the picture is more complicated because no external source is feeding correct action sequences into the focus. The action sequences have to be generated internally, they have to be evaluated as to their desirability, and they have to be stored in memory in a way that makes desirable actions likely to be carried out in the future and undesirable ones likely to be avoided. In advanced learning of actions, nearly correct sequences of actions are fed into the focus from memory by recall of actions of role models. This corresponds to one person's adopting another person's speech patterns, mannerisms, facial expressions, ways of walking, and so forth; it will be discussed below in the section on social learning.

Initial Conditions for Learning How does a human being or an animal decide whether a sequence of actions is desirable or undesirable? For some things critical to survival the answer is simple: We are born with preferences and dislikes and with instinctive ways to act; they are built in. For example, the preference for a proper blood-sugar level and body temperature need not be learned, nor does the dislike of hot or cold or of excessive pressure on the skin. To be more exact, they need not be learned by the individual; the learning has been done by the species in millions of years of evolution and is now passed on to the individual as a part of its genetic endowment. Likewise, animals have automatic reflexes, such as the sucking reflex of infant mammals. Given that there are such desirable and undesirable (subjective) states, we can define desirable and undesirable action sequences according to the states to which they lead.

To relate such built-in preferences to our model, we require that *some states (i.e., patterns in the focus) are inherently good and others are inherently bad*, with most states being indifferent. Rational action then means that the system will choose actions that lead toward good states and away from bad ones, and learning to act means that the system will store in memory sequences of actions in a way that increases the likelihood of finding good states and of avoiding bad ones.

Another condition for learning has already been mentioned, namely, that the system must *generate action sequences on its own* and store them in memory for later use. These constitute material for selection. To choose favorable ones among the sequences, the system must also *evaluate action sequences*. In what follows I will discuss several ways of finding good action sequences and of avoiding bad ones.

Let me start by expressing the learning problem mathematically. The system's (subjective) state at a particular time is given by the pattern in the system's focus at that time. The system has a (scalar) *preference function* defined on its subjective states; it is a function on patterns. The good and bad states occupy regions of the pattern space, with the good regions corresponding to high (positive) values and relative maxima of the preference function and the bad regions corresponding to low (negative) values and relative minima of that function. Were the system able to move in the state space, it would seek the relative maxima.

The indifferent states can acquire value according to whether they are found on paths to desirable or undesirable states. Learning to act can then be looked at as assigning preferences to states that start out as indifferent states. Formally, the built-in preference function maps patterns in the focus to (scalar) preference values. For most patterns the value of the function is near zero (meaning indifferent), and learning means assigning positive and negative values to more and more indifferent patterns. Learning to act then means extending positive and negative preferences to patterns with action components in a way that increases the likelihood of actions leading to desirable states and decreases the likelihood of actions leading to undesirable states.

Learning by Trial and Error   As was stated above, to learn to act the system must generate action sequences on its own. That is, it must generate patterns in the part of the focus that controls the system's motors. The initial generation of actions could be random, corresponding to the thrashing about of infants. Whatever follows these actions, including the effects of the actions, is then fed into the focus by the system's senses. In this way, action-effect pairs (or, more precisely, sensation-action pairs) will appear in the focus, from which they can be stored in memory.

A very simple way to learn is to observe the present situation, generate a random action, observe the resulting situation, and record it all in memory. As a consequence, the memory builds a model of the world that includes also the effects of the system's own actions. The memory can then be used to predict consequences of proposed actions—that is, to plan. Planning would proceed as follows: If the present situation resembles strongly a past one, the system can propose an action by whatever means it has (e.g., by recall from memory or by random generation). The situation and the proposed action together are then used to recall a resulting situation in the past (see the preceding section). If that situation had an action associated with it in the past, further iterations can be made to plan further into the future. If such iterations result in a favorable situation as determined by the system's preference function, the system has a reason to proceed with the proposed action; if it results in an unfavorable situation, the system should try another action. We are assuming that in planning of this kind the system can block off external input after accepting the initial input (the present situation) and that it can suspend the execution of actions until it has accepted some proposed action.

A learning scheme of this kind is reasonable if the repertoire of situations and actions (the system's state space) is small and simple, or if the proportion of desirable states among all possible states is large. Under such circumstances, favorable actions could be found with reasonable speed. The systems that are of interest here, however, have very large and complex state spaces with relatively few desirable states, and consequently this learning method is much too slow to be of practical interest. The situation is familiar from artificial intelligence: Systems based on simple searching cannot cope rapidly with complex situations.

The efficiency of searching and learning can be improved considerably if good paths are remembered and are used later to find inherently good states. The method corresponds to backtracking search, and it works as follows: If the effects of a (possibly random) sequence of actions are good in a situation—that is, if an action sequence leads to a desirable pattern in the system's focus—the sequence leading to that pattern is considered to be good. To make use of that discovery later, the positive preference is extended backward, with decreasing intensity, to the patterns leading to the desirable one, and the sequence of patterns (or situation-action pairs) is written in memory. A positive value of the preference function then comes to mean either that the present pattern is inherently good or that a path from the present pattern to an inherently good one—a sequence of actions—has been found and stored in memory. Extending the preference thus improves the system's ability to detect sequences that are likely to lead to a good outcome. Similar ideas are found in Holland's work on classifier systems, in which credit for a good outcome is apportioned among active classifiers according to a "bucket brigade" algorithm, increasing the probability of a good outcome in the future (Holland 1986; Holland et al. 1986).

Likewise, negative preference can be extended backward to patterns leading to an undesirable pattern. In addition, the undesirable sequences themselves can be stored in memory—although they need not, because, by definition, it is not important for the system to find states that are inherently bad. If the sequences are not stored, the system will still be able to avoid undesirable states, but it will not be able to retrace the steps to an inherently bad state and hence to determine the reason for avoiding a particular state.

Realizing the Preference Function A mechanism for storing patterns in memory was described in detail in chapter 7. The same mechanism can be used for storing the preference function, which is a scalar function on patterns: The value of the function can be stored the way a pattern component is. Thus, each memory location would have a counter for the preference function. If the address of the memory location is a favorable pattern, the counter will be positive; if it is an unfavorable pattern, the counter will be negative; and if it is indifferent or as yet undefined, the counter will be close to zero.

In reading from the memory, the counters for the preference function can be pooled in the same way as are the counters for a pattern component, and their sum tells whether the pattern in the focus is favorable (sum greater than zero) or unfavorable (sum less than zero). Having a built-in preference function then means that the function counters of some locations are nonzero from the start and that such nonzero counters may even be unmodifiable. Extending the preference means taking the present value of the function (especially if it is strongly positive or negative), reducing it toward zero, and writing it into the function counters of locations activated by the most recent patterns of the sequence, together with the writing of the sequence itself.

Speed of Learning The learning methods described so far are basic, in that they allow a system to learn even if it is left alone. However, these methods are slow, and therefore behavior based on such learning is not rich and complicated. This does not mean that animals growing up in isolation cannot have complicated behaviors, only that any such behaviors they do have are prewired or preprogrammed genetically. Rigidity is typical of such behavior; the behavior is automatic. A standard stimulus elicits a standard response, no matter how inappropriate to the particular situation it may be (e.g., in experimental situations that imitate nature in some significant ways but differ from it in others).

Learning in Social Settings

Let us take a cursory look at learning theory, to see how some well-known results could be accounted for by the memory model. The common thread is that an individual learns from a trainer or a role model.

In competition for survival, fast learning is advantageous. Learning from others speeds up learning dramatically and makes possible the learning of complex behaviors (which can be quite arbitrary). This is most evident in human learning. Knowing how to swim is useful in almost any society, but it is unlikely that most of us would learn without a teacher or an example. Language is a learned skill that is very complex and in many ways arbitrary. Different languages involve very different vocabularies, different ways of making sounds, different grammars, and different systems of writing, and yet they perform very similar communication tasks. The behavior survives by being learned, practiced, and taught.

Classical Conditioning In classical conditioning (also called Pavlovian learning or supervised learning), an artificial (new) stimulus is substituted for a natural (old) one. The natural or old stimulus is one for which the subject already has a (natural or old) response, and the artificial or new stimulus is one for which the subject has no response. By training, the subject learns to give the old response to the new stimulus. The training goes as follows: The trainer presents a new stimulus (e.g., a bell) followed by an old stimulus (food). The subject responds (salivation). After sufficient repetition, the new stimulus alone will elicit the old response; the old response has become *associated* with the new stimulus. However, if the two stimuli are presented in the other order, old before new (food before bell), there is no learning; the new stimulus will not elicit the old response.

To relate this to the memory model, notice that the old or natural stimulus is meaningful to the subject at the start of the experiment but the new or artificial is not. In terms of the model, this means that the system's preference has been established for patterns representing the old stimulus but not for patterns representing the new stimulus. Thus, when the subject receives the old stimulus, it also encounters a nonzero value of the preference function. This tells the memory to store the sequence of patterns leading to the old stimulus and to extend the preference to those patterns. If the new stimulus precedes the old stimulus repeatedly, the sequence leading from the new stimulus to the old response becomes established in memory and the preference function likewise becomes established for that sequence. Consequently, the new stimulus alone will produce the old response, and it can even take the place of the old stimulus in training another artificial stimulus for the old response.

What if, instead, the new stimulus is presented after the old stimulus but before the old response? Will the old response become associated with the new stimulus? Psychological experiments have shown that, as a rule, it does not. An explanation, based on the memory model, would be as follows: The association from the old stimulus to the old response has already been formed, and the preference has been extended to the old stimulus, so that there is no sudden change in preference when the old response is given, and thus no learning is initiated by this mechanism.

In summary: Classical conditioning makes use of reward and punishment—that is, things that are inherently good or bad or that have in the past been associated with good or bad things—to teach the subject specific behavior patterns, which can be quite arbitrary. Possible memory mechanisms at work here are the recording of meaningful experiences and the extending of preferences to previously indifferent states.

Learning by Imitation   The most complex forms of learned behavior, such as the use of language, are acquired largely by imitating other individuals. What learning mechanisms might be at work there?

So far I have proposed two occasions for a system to learn: when an unexpected event takes place, and when a meaningful event takes place. An event is *unexpected* if the memory provides a clear prediction for it but the prediction is incorrect. The memory record is then considered to be at fault and is modified so as to improve prediction under similar conditions in the future. The occasion of learning is thus the same as in the failure-driven memory of Schank (1982). An event is *meaningful* if it fetches a strongly positive or negative value of the system's preference function. The sequence leading to the meaningful event is then stored in memory, and the preference is extended back to the last few patterns of the sequence.

The two occasions for learning can be combined into one if success and failure in predicting are meaningful in themselves. Let us assume that when the memory makes a good prediction the system experiences it as a positive value of the preference function, and that when it makes a bad prediction the system experiences it as a negative value. In both cases the just-preceding sequence of events is written (again) in memory and the preference is extended back to the sequence. A system of this kind will learn from mistakes but will take time to build confidence in what it has thus learned; in general, it prefers and tends toward predictable things.

It seems that an internal reward mechanism of this kind is necessary if a system is to learn by imitation. In addition, a second internal ingredient seems to be necessary: The system must use itself to model the behavior of other systems. Successful modeling is then experienced as a positive thing. This may sound like a fancy way of saying that to learn by imitation one must like imitating, but there is more to it when we relate it to the memory model. First, the system must store an image of the behavior of others; second, it must map this image onto actions of its own; third, it must observe the results of its own actions and compare them against its image of the behavior of other (that is, the system must *identify* with the role model). Because of its internal reward mechanism, the system works to perfect the match between its own behavior and that of the role model.

It is my assumption that such internal mechanisms, including internal reward and punishment, are behind learning by imitation, which, in turn, is primarily responsible for complicated social learning (external reward and punishment being only secondarily responsible). Through social learning, groups of individuals can develop and maintain behavior patterns that have very little to do with an individual's survival in an indifferent environment. In fact, a group's behavior can produce a new environment that is maintained by the behavior. Diverse civilizations and cultures provide numerous examples of this. They are based largely on the models people have and the modeling they do in their heads. The study of such modeling is a major research task and will not be undertaken here.

Application to the Frame Problem of Robotics

The organization of an autonomous system discussed in this chapter has been motivated by observations about the organization of information processing in animals. It should therefore help us think of how to build robots, and it should shed light on outstanding problems in robotics. The *frame problem* is one such problem that has been discussed widely in the artificial-intelligence community (Pylyshyn 1987). It deals with the updating of a robot's internal model of the world as the robot interacts with the world—that is, how a robot can keep a tally of the side effects of contemplated actions. The following example illustrates the problem.

A robot lives in a world. To function there, the robot maintains an internal model of the world—a data base. In the data base are represented objects of the world (e.g., the robot, a cart, a telephone, room 1, room 2), properties of the objects (e.g., all rooms are stationary, the cart is movable, the telephone is blue), and relations between objects (e.g., the cart is in room 1, the telephone is on the cart, the telephone's receiver is on the hook). To allow the robot to plan actions, the world model must specify the ways in which things interact when the robot acts on the world—say, when it moves the cart from room 1 to room 2. What, besides the cart (and the robot), will end up in room 2? What entries in the data base, other than the ones for the cart and the robot, must be updated? Naturally, what must be updated are the entries for all the things resting on the cart (i.e., the telephone) except those tied by a short cord to the wall (again, the telephone), since they (and things resting on them) will fall on the floor of room 1 and thus will no longer be on the cart (nor will the receiver be on the hook). The story can be made as complicated as one wishes, and that is the source of the frame problem.

Why is this not problematic for humans or animals? An easy answer is that humans and animals have *common sense*, which robots lack, and this common sense has been gained through *experience*. But how does common sense work? How is experience acquired, and how is it used?

Most of this chapter has been about that very issue. The world model in the memory has been built from exposure to the world, that is, from experience. The statistical regularities of the world, including the system's own actions and their effects, are an integral part of the model. That means that not just the main effects of actions but also the side effects are recorded in memory. A system without experience cannot predict at all, and one with a lot of experience can produce comprehensive predictions. Therefore, by virtue of how the world model comes to be and how it works, it provides answers to what else might happen (e.g., when the robot pushes the cart from room 1 to room 2), much as a scale model of a physical object can provide answers about the behavior of the real object.

This gives rise to two comments, one about a scale model in the head and the other about the seriousness of the entire enterprise.

The idea of a scale model in the head may seem bizarre at first. Are there supposed to be tiny cats and dogs and trains and robots and telephones with cords, all in the head? Not at all, but there are *patterns* of activation of neurons *caused by those objects*. When the real objects are in front of us, they, too, are available to us only as patterns produced by our senses. These patterns are the objects that the brain deals with—not the objects themselves. The memory record is constructed from these very patterns, and the memory reproduces them in the focus more or less faithfully when properly cued. Thus, what the memory reproduces in the conscious part of the mind is of the same nature as what the senses produced there from the real stuff out in the world.

Let us turn to modeling in the physical world and look at the relationship between a physical object and a physical model of it. Let us assume that we want to find out what happens when two trains crash head-on. We can, of course, run the experiment with real trains and see what happens. The information would be reliable, but getting a large sample would be very expensive. A less expensive alternative is to build scale models of trains, run the experiment on them, and see what happens. Much could be learned from this, although the information would not be fully reliable because scale models do not behave in exactly the same way as their real counterparts.

Similarly with the real world and the world model stored in memory: We can establish a set of initial conditions in the world, let the world turn, and see or experience what the consequences are, or we can imagine a set of initial conditions, let the memory turn, and see or experience what consequences it produces. The more experienced the individual, the more faithful the world model and the better the memory's prediction of the consequences. In that sense, then, there *is* a scale model in the head: It produces in us experiences of the same nature as does the real world.

But who or what interprets the model; who or what interprets what comes out of the memory? The question can be answered indirectly: It is whoever or whatever interprets the world. A direct answer would be more satisfactory, but for that, instead of asking *who* or *what interprets*, it is better to ask *how* the model, or the world, *gets interpreted* by the whoever. Furthermore, we need to look at the meaning of the word 'interpret'.

The interpretation of a signal, a situation, or a message by a subject manifests itself in the reaction that the thing evokes in the subject. The reaction can be internal or external, 'internal' meaning subjective experience (pleasure, pain, emotion, association, propensity to act—the things that we call 'mental') and 'external' meaning action (e.g., dodging a fastball). We judge the correctness of an interpretation by how appropriate the subjective experience or the triggered action is to the conditions causing it. If it is inappropriate, we say that the subject does not understand the situation or the message.

Observable action involves the use of the muscles. Some actions are wired in as automatic reflexes; others are learned. The learned ones are of interest to us here. In the section on learning to act, we considered how actions can become associated with external cues. For present purposes, the important thing is that the patterns from which the world model is constructed include components for action. When the memory reproduces patterns in the focus, the action components of these patterns are ready to drive the muscles. The stored world model thus includes the system's own actions, so the system can interpret situations and messages via actions.

Subjective experience is a subtler way for a system to interpret situations and messages, but it too can be explained by the memory model. Consider the propensity to act (e.g., back-seat driving) and planning: Present or imagined cues together with the predictive power of the memory bring to consciousness (focus) possible future actions and consequences. However, the system blocks off commands to the muscles, so that there is no immediately observable action even if interpretation based on the world model is going on within. In that sense, subjective experience is just as real a way to interpret situations and messages as is action.

Finally, there are the most basic forms of interpretation. With animals and humans, some things have meaning in themselves and can thus be interpreted without further learning. The experiencing of certain things as pleasurable or painful, and possibly some emotions, are handed down genetically. We have modeled them with the built-in preference function, which gives basic meaning to the world.

In the paragraphs above we have considered only the very basics of interpretation and meaning, but these basics appear to operate in all intelligent beings. With higher animals, and with humans in particular, social learning is exceedingly important, and the resulting web of interpretations and meanings becomes very complex. Even then, the *mechanisms* of interpretation and meaning can be few and simple, akin to those discussed above, with the complexity arising from the infinity of ways in which the mechanisms allow new meanings to be derived from old ones.

We can now attempt to say who interprets the world or the world model: The individual does. And what is the individual? A composite of sensors and motors, possessing a built-in preference function for some sensory patterns and capable of building from its own sensations and actions a world model for future reference. The preference function and the world model or memory are the means by which the individual interprets, and the motors allow interpretations to be expressed externally.

The second comment is about the seriousness of this approach overall. Can traditional artificial-intelligence methods be replaced with a memory that somehow produces right answers automatically? Can there be such a memory? First, it is not clear that one method has to replace the other, although it is quite clear that the traditional methods alone are in trouble. Second, the memory is mathematically sound and easily built from neuronlike components, and it does not guarantee right answers any more than biological memories do. Third, the retrieval properties, including the ways in which the memory fails, are lifelike, regardless of the extreme simplicity of the model.

Since nature *has* solved the frame problem, we should be able to solve it by understanding how information processing is organized in animals. To the extent that the memory model captures that organization, it is relevant to the solution of the problem. The position taken here is that the memory, as I have modeled it, contributes to the solution significantly, and that an equally significant contribution is made by the sensory system that prepares information for the memory. Thus, a major part of the burden is on the sensory system. That part is the topic of the next section.

The Encoding Problem

The sensors of the various modalities collectively receive a mass of stimuli of a specific type, and from it they derive patterns for processing by the nervous system. From these patterns the brain builds its model of the world. As the model learns to reproduce regularities of the world, it allows the system to predict and to contemplate the consequences of its own actions, making it possible for the system to plan.

The raw signal arriving at the sense organs is ill suited for building a predictive model. Even if a number of regularities of the world are present in the signal, they appear in far-from-optimal form and are embedded in noise. A cursory look at raw speech waves, for example, makes one wonder how anything of importance can be extracted from them; the waves for the same word spoken by different people can look very different. A sensory system thus has two functions: to filter out noise and to transform relevant information into a form that is useful in building and using the world model.

Transforming the input signal into a form useful for modeling the world is referred to here as the *encoding problem*. In my model for an autonomous system, the encoding task falls on the sensory system, which is assisted by memory. For an example, let us take vision in our three-dimensional world inhabited by various kinds of objects. The world model needs encodings of those objects, and the visual system has to produce the encodings. From how the memory works we can derive requirements for a good visual encoding. Since patterns stored in memory attract similar patterns, the memory chunks things with similar encodings, forming objects and individuals from them. On the other hand, the retinal image of an object varies widely according to the distance between the object and the viewer; yet those very different images should produce very similar encodings. The job of the visual system, then, is to express the retinal image in features that are relatively insensitive to scale, among other things. Similarly, to understand the speech of different individuals having vocal cords of different length, the auditory system needs to express the audio signal in features that are relatively insensitive to absolute pitch, among other things. Similar remarks can be made for the other senses.

Often a given input signal can be encoded in several different ways, and yet we seem to have only one interpretation of it at a time. How we perceive the Necker cube is an example of this, as the interpretations of our looking at it from above and from below flip back and forth. This can be attributed to assistance or feedback from memory. If the sensory system can produce an encoding of something familiar, it tends to do so. Note that familiarity implies memory.

Once the objects of the world have been encoded properly, a sparse distributed memory can form a dynamic model of the world from the encoded objects. The model will then let us examine the effects, direct and indirect, of contemplated actions in the same way—that is, with the same machinery—as we, as observers of the world, examine the effects of real actions.

This solution to the frame problem is truly a solution only if we can solve the encoding problem. The likelihood of that depends on how good our model of an autonomous system is, and that in turn depends on how well it captures the essence of how animals are organized. It seems to me that solving the frame problem will require much work, and much of the work has to be devoted to the understanding of sensory systems. In that work, the models of the memory and of an autonomous learning system can serve as valuable guides.

Related Work Our picture here of an autonomous system and of the encoding of sensory data is extremely simple. Grossberg's (1980) paper on the formation of a stable cognitive code goes into the subject more deeply. That paper and Albus' (1981) book emphasize the hierarchical organization of intelligent systems. The autonomous systems of the present chapter are roughly equivalent to a single layer in a hierarchy proposed by Albus.

Anderson (1986) and Anderson and Murphy (1986) have emphasized the crucial role of the encoded form of information—that is, the actual representation itself rather than what an encoding represents. (The importance of representation is also appreciated in the field of artificial intelligence, but usually only high-level representations are considered, as in the problem of covering an 8 × 8 board with 1 × 2 domino pieces after a pair of diagonally opposite corner squares have been removed.) Their work and mine suggest that we need to mind the representations at the very lowest levels, and that representations of at least some higher-level concepts might be derived by mechanically combining the encodings of lower-level concepts. Furthermore, it is of utmost importance that the representations be suited for highly parallel computation; at least this is so for brains, which are made of relatively slow neurons.

Traditional artificial intelligence is modeled on how humans reason and how they describe their thinking and their problem solving. These phenomena are at the highest, most conscious levels of human behavior, and are rather serial in nature. Artificial-intelligence methods perform poorly on tasks (such as pattern recognition) that happen at lower levels and that are, from the subjective point of view, automatic. In my memory model, serial phenomena and pattern recognition have very different statuses. Serial phenomena are modeled by stored associations between patterns—that is, by pointer chains—whereas the memory's power for pattern recognition comes from the metric properties of the pattern space, which the memory exploits. However, even serial recall is based on the recognition of patterns and on the convergence of iterated reading to stored patterns and sequences. Thus, the geometry of the pattern space, or the structure of the symbols, determines many properties of the memory. It seems, then, that artificial-intelligence methods need to be augmented with mathematical and statistical methods of dealing with representations in high-dimensional spaces. Thus, in addition to symbolic structures we need to study the structure of symbols. This point is made emphatically in Hofstadter 1985—see, in particular, chapter 26, "Waking Up from the Boolean Dream."

Summary and Conclusions

In this book I have developed a model of memory that captures some basic properties of human long-term memory. Although human memory is much more complicated than my model of it or the models of others, it is essential to understand simple models of the right kind before we can hope to develop more comprehensive models and to understand the full phenomenon of memory. The sparse-distributed-memory model is offered in that spirit.

In my modeling, very large patterns of features encode moments of experience, and sequences of such patterns model sequences of events that occur over time. Because the patterns stored in memory can also be used to address the memory, sequences can be stored as pointer chains. Any pattern in a sequence, or a sufficiently similar pattern, can then be used to retrieve the rest of the sequence. The sequences can be arbitrarily long, because the capacity of the memory can be made arbitrarily large by making the number of storage locations sufficiently large. Simple pointer chains cannot handle crossings of sequences. For sequence crossings, the memory model has multiple folds, each associated with its own delay parameter.

Memory plays but a part (though an important part) in human cognition: It stores a dynamic, predictive model of the world. Another part is the extraction of information from the world and the encoding of it before it is stored. That part is carried out by the senses of sight, hearing, touch, and the other senses, with assistance from memory. My treatment of sensory systems has been very general and can be summarized as follows: The memory works with features and creates its internal objects and individuals by chunking together things that are similar in terms of those features. In order for those internal objects to match objects of the world, the system's sensors must transform raw input from the world into features that are relatively invariant over small perturbations of objects. To recall a stored "object," the senses—or the memory—must produce a reasonable approximation of the encoding that was used as an address when the object was stored.

Yet another part of human cognition has to do with action as a way of affecting the world. Actions are carried out by motors or muscles. My modeling of motor systems has been very general and abstract, the main point being that the motors are controlled by sequences of patterns that can be stored in memory.

I have combined these ideas in a simple model of an autonomous learning system. The system has a central place, the *focus*, that accounts for the system's subjective experience. The entity in the focus is a very large pattern, a high-dimensional vector of features that encodes everything about that moment (that is, any specific things that the system may be attending to, the system's action, and the overall context). The memory is addressed by the focus, the memory's output goes into the focus, the senses feed into the focus, and the muscles are driven from the focus. This architecture is motivated by the oneness of subjective experience; an experience created by the senses can also be created by the memory. The system's modeling of the world is founded on this idea.

A system with such an architecture seems capable of learning how the world works and of learning how its own actions affect the world (including how they affect its own well-being). The well-being is modeled by a built-in preference function that is defined on the states of the focus. In learning to act, the system needs to store favorable action sequences in memory and to assign positive and negative preferences to previously indifferent states. In the most advanced form of learning, namely imitation, the system uses itself to model the behavior of others of its kind.

Besides possibly helping us understand human and animal memory, the present research suggests a way to build a new kind of computer memory: a random-access memory for very long words with approximate addressing. To use such a memory in robots, we have to learn to encode information about the world and about motor action into high-dimensional feature vectors. Major research topics for the future thus include sensory encoding, motor action, and memory storage. These three topics entail very different problems, all of which will have to be solved if we are to build robots that can operate with any reasonable degree of autonomy.

Appendix A
The Distribution of the Third Side of a Triangle

THEOREM The distribution of the length c of the third side of a triangle of $\{0, 1\}^n$, with the other two sides of length a and b, resembles the binomial distribution with the parameters n and p, with $p = a/n + b/n - 2(a/n)(b/n)$.

Proof Consider the triangle $\{0, A, B\}$ of N, $N = \{0, 1\}^n$, where A and B are random points of N satisfying $|A| = a$ and $|B| = b$. The length c of the third side is then the distance from A to B, $c = d(A, B) = |A - B|$.

The idea of the proof is the following: First, the difference $A - B$ has ones whenever A and B disagree, and hence the ones occur with probability

$$[(n - a)/n](b/n) + (a/n)[(n - b)/n],$$

which equals p; second, since A and B are random points, the n bits of their difference are nearly independent. Hence the distribution is approximately binomial with parameters n and p.

Formally, let the coordinates of A be $\langle a_0, \ldots, a_{n-1} \rangle$. Then the length a is the sum of the coordinates,

$$a = |A| = a_0 + \cdots + a_{n-1}.$$

Similarly,

$$B = \langle b_0, \ldots, b_{n-1} \rangle,$$

and

$$b = |B| = b_0 + \cdots + b_{n-1}.$$

The length c can then be expressed as the sum

$$c = |A - B| = |a_0 - b_0| + \cdots + |a_{n-1} - b_{n-1}| = c_0 + \cdots + c_{n-1}.$$

A component of the sum, c_i, is 1 if and only if the ith coordinates of A and B differ.

Now estimate the number of ones in $A - B$. A coordinate of A is 1 with probability a/n, and so its mean is given by

$$E\{a_i\} = \Pr\{a_i = 1\} = a/n.$$

Similarly,
$$E\{b_i\} = b/n.$$

Since A and B are random points of N, the variables $\{a_i\}$ are independent of the variables $\{b_i\}$. The expectation of c_i is then given by

$$\begin{aligned} p &= E\{c_i\} \\ &= \Pr\{c_i = 1\} \\ &= \Pr\{(a_i = 0 \ \& \ b_i = 1) \lor (a_i = 1 \ \& \ b_i = 0)\} \\ &= \Pr\{a_i = 0 \ \& \ b_i = 1\} + \Pr\{a_i = 1 \ \& \ b_i = 0\}, \end{aligned}$$

which, by independence, is equal to

$$\Pr\{a_i = 0\} \cdot \Pr\{b_i = 1\} + \Pr\{a_i = 1\} \cdot \Pr\{b_i = 0\}$$

$$= \frac{n-a}{n}\frac{b}{n} + \frac{a}{n}\frac{n-b}{n}$$

$$= a/n + b/n - 2(a/n)(b/n),$$

which is the value for p as stated by the theorem. For the mean length of the third side, we then have

$$\begin{aligned} E\{c\} &= E\{c_0 + \cdots + c_{n-1}\} \\ &= np \\ &= a + b - 2ab/n. \end{aligned}$$

To estimate the variance of the third side, $\mathrm{Var}\{c\}$, notice that the terms of c (the variables $\{c_i\} = \{|a_i - b_i|\}$) are nearly independent. A slight dependence is due to the requirements that A have exactly a ones and that B have exactly b ones; hence, only certain values of $|A - B|$ are possible. Assuming independence, the bits of the difference $A - B$ are n independent $\{0, 1\}$ (Bernoulli) variables, each with probability p of being 1, and hence

$$\mathrm{Var}\{c\} \cong npq,$$

where $p = a/n + b/n - 2(a/n)(b/n)$, as above, and $q = 1 - p$.

The exact variance can be derived as follows: First, $\mathrm{Var}\{c\} = E\{c^2\} - E^2\{c\}$. For $E\{c^2\}$ we can write

$$\begin{aligned} E\{c^2\} &= E \sum_{i,j} c_i c_j \\ &= E \sum_i c_i^2 + E \sum_{i \neq j} c_i c_j \\ &= n E\{c_i^2\} + n(n-1) E\{c_i c_j\}. \end{aligned}$$

Since $c_i \,(= |a_i - b_i|)$ is either 0 or 1, we have $E\{c_i^2\} = E\{c_i\} = p$. For $i \neq j$ the expectation $E\{c_i c_j\}$ becomes

$$E\{c_i c_j\} = \Pr\{c_i c_j = 1\}$$
$$= \Pr\{a_i \neq b_i \,\&\, a_j \neq b_j\}$$
$$= \Pr\{\langle a_i, b_i, a_j, b_j \rangle \in \{\langle 1, 0, 1, 0\rangle, \langle 1, 0, 0, 1\rangle,$$
$$\langle 0, 1, 1, 0\rangle, \langle 0, 1, 0, 1\rangle\}\}$$

$$= \frac{a}{n}\frac{n-b}{n}\frac{a-1}{n-1}\frac{n-b-1}{n-1}$$
$$+ \frac{a}{n}\frac{n-b}{n}\frac{n-a}{n-1}\frac{b}{n-1} + \frac{n-a}{n}\frac{b}{n}\frac{a}{n-1}\frac{n-b}{n-1}$$
$$+ \frac{n-a}{n}\frac{b}{n}\frac{n-a-1}{n-1}\frac{b-1}{n-1}$$

$$= [a(a-1)(n-b)(n-b-1)$$
$$+ 2a(n-b)(n-a)b + (n-a)(n-a-1)b(b-1)]$$
$$/[n^2(n-1)^2].$$

Assuming that neither A nor B is near the origin or its complement, $0 \ll a, b \ll n$, we can round off the five -1's into zeros and get the estimate

$$E\{c_i c_j\} \cong \{[a(n-b)]^2 + 2a(n-b)(n-a)b + [(n-a)b]^2\}/n^4$$
$$= [a(n-b) + (n-a)b]^2/n^4$$
$$= [n(a+b) - 2ab]^2/n^4$$
$$= p^2,$$

where $p = E\{c_i\} = a/n + b/n - 2(a/n)(b/n)$, as above. The variance of the third side then becomes

$$\text{Var}\{c\} = E\{c^2\} - E^2\{c\}$$
$$= n[E\{c_i^2\} + (n-1)E\{c_i c_j\}] - E^2\{c\}$$
$$\cong n[p + (n-1)p^2] - (np)^2$$
$$= np(1-p)$$
$$= npq,$$

which is what we had before, satisfying the theorem.

How does the distribution "resemble" the binomial distribution? It is discrete, and for the parameters n and p it has a mean np, as does the binomial, and a variance that is approximately npq (the binomial's is exactly npq). The big difference is in the range of values for the two distributions. The binomial's range is $0, 1, 2, \ldots, n$, whereas the third side of a triangle can have only values $|a - b|, |a - b| + 2, |a - b| + 4, \ldots$ up to the smaller of $|a + b|$ and n (or $n - 1$ instead of n if $n - |a - b|$ is odd). However, the nonzero probabilities for the length of the third side are approximately twice the binomial probabilities, and if n is large and the lengths of the two known sides are reasonably close to $n/2$, the approximation is extremely good. The exact probabilities can be derived from the hypergeometric distribution (Feller 1957). □

Appendix B
The Intersection of Two Circles

In Chapter 7 we need to measure the intersection of two circles. The measure is used to determine whether a previously stored item can be recovered from memory. The size of the intersection is derived here by finding the size of the set difference of two circles, called the lune; the size of the intersection is then the size of the circle minus the size of the lune. Only the case where the radii of the two circles are equal will be discussed.

If X is the circle with center x and radius r, then $X = O(r, x)$. Similarly, if Y is the circle $O(r, y)$, then the *lune* $Q(r, x, y)$ is the set of points of X that are outside Y, or

$$Q(r, x, y) = X \backslash Y$$
$$= O(r, x) \backslash O(r, y)$$
$$= \{z \mid d(x, z) \leq r \ \& \ d(y, z) > r\}.$$

The area of the lune is the number of points in $Q(r, x, y)$. It is a function of the radius r and of the distance d between the centers of the two circles, $d = d(x, y)$.

THEOREM The area of the lune $\{z \mid d(x, z) \leq r \ \& \ d(y, z) > r\}$ of $\{0, 1\}^n$ is the sum of the first $d(x, y)$ terms of the series

$$\binom{0}{0}\binom{n-1}{r} + 0 + \binom{2}{1}\binom{n-3}{r-1} + 0 + \binom{4}{2}\binom{n-5}{r-2} + 0 + \cdots.$$

Proof The idea of the proof is to measure the increment in the area when the distance between the two circles (between their centers) increases by one bit. Adding up the increments as the distance grows from 0 to d gives, then, the total area of the lune.

For brevity in notation, the product xy of two points will be used for their difference (the 'exclusive or'), $xy = x \oplus y = x - y$, and hence $|xy|$ equals the distance $d(x, y)$. Assume that x is the origin, and let z and z' be two adjacent points ($|zz'| = 1$) on a minimal path from x to y, with z between x and z'. Then $0:z:z':y$ and $|z'| = |z| + 1$. In working out the

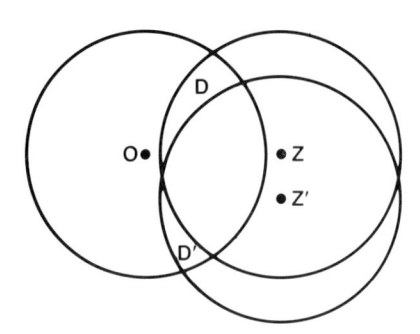

Figure B.1
Two successive lunes, $Z \setminus O$ and $Z' \setminus O$.

proof it may help to think of z as the point $1..100..00..0$ (the first $|z|$ coordinates are ones), of z' as the point $1..110..00..0$ (the first $|z|+1$ are ones), and of y as $1..111..10..0$ (the first $|y|$ are ones). For brevity, the capital letters O, Z, and Z' will be used for the circles $O(r, 0)$, $O(r, z)$, and $O(r, z')$, respectively.

Moving the center of the second circle from z to z' changes the lune from $O \setminus Z$ to $O \setminus Z'$. To determine the change in the area, $|O \setminus Z'| - |O \setminus Z|$, consider the Venn diagram of the circles O, Z, and Z' (see figure B.1) and notice how $O \setminus Z'$ differs from $O \setminus Z$: It includes $O \cap (Z \setminus Z')$ and excludes $O \cap (Z' \setminus Z)$. Call them D and D', respectively. The increase in the area due to the increase in the distance is then $|D| - |D'|$. It may seem at first that D' should be empty because z is between O and z'—that is, that no points should be removed from the lune as the second circle moves away from the first—but, as a rule, D' is nonempty.

On the next few pages we shall see that the increase in the area of the lune due to a one-bit increase in the distance is equal to the number of points of D that are exactly r bits from the origin, or $|D| - |D'| = |D_r|$, where $D_r = \{w | w \in D \ \& \ |w| = r\}$.

By definition, D can be written as

$$D = O \cap (Z \setminus Z')$$
$$= \{w | |w| \leq r \ \& \ (|wz| \leq r \ \& \ |wz'| > r)\}.$$

Because z and z' are adjacent and because of the triangle inequality, a point w of Z that is less than r bits from z is also in Z', and all of Z is within $r+1$ bits of z'. Therefore, D can be expressed as

$$D = \{w | |w| = |z| - s, \ldots, r \ \& \ |wz| = r \ \& \ |wz'| = r+1\},$$

where $s = \min\{|z|, r\}$. The condition $|w| = |z| - s, \ldots, r$ follows, by the triangle inequality, from the fact that D is a subset of $O \cap Z$. Similarly, with $s' = \min\{|z'|, r\}$,

$$D' = \{w \mid |w| = |z'| - s', \ldots, r \,\&\, |wz| = r + 1 \,\&\, |wz'| = r\}.$$

We shall now see that the lower limit of the "length" $|w|$ is $|z| - s$ for elements w of D, and it is one larger than that for elements w of D' (i.e., D is one bit closer to 0 than is D'). This is certainly true if $|z| \geq r$, for then $s = s' = r$, and $|z'| - s' = |z| + 1 - s$. So assume that $|z| < r$. Then $|z| - s = 0$. Hence, the origin could belong in D (actually it cannot when $|z| < r$, but that is not at issue here). However, the origin can never belong in D', for if it did we would have $|0z| = r + 1$ and $|0z'| = r$, contrary to $0:z:z'$. Therefore, the first conjunct in the expression for D' above can always be written as $|w| = |z'| - s, \ldots, r$, which is the same as $|w| = |z| - s + 1, \ldots, r$.

Now partition D according to the distance from the origin:

$$D = D_{|z|-s} \cup D_{|z|-s+1} \cup \cdots \cup D_r,$$

where

$$D_i = \{w \mid w \in D \,\&\, |w| = i\}$$
$$= \{w \mid |w| = i \,\&\, |wz| = r \,\&\, |wz'| = r + 1\}.$$

Similarly,

$$D' = D'_{|z|-s+1} \cup D'_{|z|-s+2} \cup \cdots \cup D'_r,$$

with

$$D'_i = \{w \mid |w| = i \,\&\, |wz| = r + 1 \,\&\, |wz'| = r\}.$$

In lemma 1 we shall see that, for $i < r$, the partitions of D and D' are pairwise equal, with $|D_i| = |D'_{i+1}|$. The difference $|D| - |D'|$ is then reduced to just $|D_r|$. The following two lemmas will help complete the proof of the theorem.

LEMMA 1
(1) $D_i = \{w \mid |w| = i \,\&\, |wz| = r \,\&\, |wz'| = r + 1\}$,
(2) $D'_i = \{w \mid |w| = i \,\&\, |wz| = r + 1 \,\&\, |wz'| = r\}$,
(3) $|zz'| = 1$, and
(4) $0:z:z'$

imply

(5) $|D_i| = |D'_{i+1}|$.

Proof It suffices to show that multiplication (exclusive or) by zz' maps D_i one to one onto D'_{i+1}. Since the 'exclusive or' is a one-to-one mapping, we need to show only that the mapping is onto. The proof is based on the facts that one coordinate in D_i is 0 and the same coordinate in D'_{i+1} is 1 and that this coordinate is indicated by the sole 1 bit of zz' ($|zz'| = 1$).

Assuming that w is in D_i, we need to show that wzz' is in D'_{i+1}. The second and third conditions of line (2) of the lemma are easy: According to (1), $|(wzz')z| = |wz'| = r + 1$ and $|(wzz')z'| = |wz| = r$. So it remains to be shown that $|wzz'| = i + 1$.

The conditions $|wz| = r$, $|zz'| = 1$, and $|wz'| = r + 1$ mean that z is between w and z', $w:z:z'$, which, when multiplied by zz', becomes $wzz':z':z$, allowing us to extend $w:z:z'$ into $w:z:z':wzz'$. The distance between the endpoints w and wzz' is 1, and that between the middle points z and z' is also 1. Now consider the place where w differs from wzz' and where z differs from z'. It is indicated by the single 1 bit of zz'. Let it be the kth coordinate, so that $w_k \neq (wzz')_k$ and $z_k \neq z'_k$.

We now see that the kth bit of w is 0, that the kth bit of wzz' is 1, and that therefore wzz' is in D'_{i+1}: Because z is between 0 and z', $0:z:z'$, their kth bits are in a like relation, $0:z_k:z'_k$. If the kth bit of z were 1, we would have $0:1:0$, which is false, so $z_k = 0$ and $z'_k = 1$. From $w:z:z':wzz'$ we get that $w_k:z_k:z'_k:(wzz')_k$, which must be $0:0:1:1$, as $1:0:1:0$ is false, so $w_k = 0$ and $(wzz')_k = 1$. Since the only difference between w and wzz' is the kth bit and since that is 1 in wzz', we get that $|wzz'| = |w| + 1 = i + 1$, which completes the proof that wzz' is in D'_{i+1}.

The proof of lemma 1 thus far shows that, for some k, the elements of D_i have the kth bit equal to 0, and that they become elements of D'_{i+1} by changing the bit to 1. Similarly, zz' maps D'_{i+1} to D_i by changing the kth bit from 1 to 0. The details of this second half of the proof are omitted. The result is that zz' is a one-to-one mapping of D_i onto D'_{i+1}, and hence $|D_i| = |D'_{i+1}|$. □

LEMMA 2
(1) $D_r = \{w | |w| = r \ \& \ |wz| = r \ \& \ |wz'| = r + 1\}$,
(2) $|zz'| = 1$, and
(3) $j = |z'| = |z| + 1$

imply

(4) $|D_r| = \begin{cases} \binom{j-1}{(j-1)/2}\binom{n-j}{r-(j-1)/2} & \text{if } j \text{ is odd,} \\ 0 & \text{otherwise.} \end{cases}$

Proof From (1) and (2) it follows that some (kth) coordinate of all w in D_r is 0 ($w_k = 0$; see proof of lemma 1). Therefore, D_r is a subset of an $(n-1)$-dimensional subspace of $\{0,1\}^n$, and so our task is to count the $(n-1)$-tuples w that satisfy $|w| = |wz| = r$, according to (1), and $|z| = j - 1$, according to (3). For w to be r bits from z (since $|wz| = r$) it must have some number u of zeros where z has its $j - 1$ ones and some number v of ones where z has its $n - j$ zeros, with $u + v = |wz| = r$. The number of such $(n - 1)$-tuples is $(j - 1 : u)(n - j : v)$. The number of ones in w is $(j - 1 - u) + v$, which, according to (1), must equal r. Solving $u + v = r$ and $(j - 1 - u) + v = r$ for u and v gives $u = (j - 1)/2$ and $v = r - (j - 1)/2$, which are integers only if j is odd. Substituting for u and v in $|D_r| = (j - 1 : u)(r - j : v)$ finally gives (4). □

To complete the proof of the theorem, use a sequence of $d + 1$ circles, $d = d(x, y)$, all with radius r, from $O(r, x)$ to $O(r, y)$, with their centers along a minimal path from x to y—$\langle O(r, z(j)) \rangle$ $(j = 0, \ldots, d)$, $z(0) = x$, $z(d) = y$, $d(z(j), z(j + 1)) = 1$, and $x:z(j):z(j + 1)$—and add the increments $|D_r|$ for $j = 1, \ldots, d$. □

The following two corollaries come from two ways of computing the size of a circle:

COROLLARY 1a For $r < n/2$,

$$\binom{0}{0}\binom{n-1}{r} + \binom{2}{1}\binom{n-3}{r-1} + \binom{4}{2}\binom{n-5}{r-2} + \cdots$$
$$+ \binom{2r}{r}\binom{n-2r-1}{0}$$
$$= \binom{n}{0} + \binom{n}{1} + \binom{n}{2} + \cdots + \binom{n}{r}.$$

Proof In the theorem, let the distance d between the centers of the two circles be $2r + 1$. (See figure B.2.) Then the circles no longer intersect, and the lune is all of the circle $O(r, x)$. Finally, $|O(r, x)| = (n : 0) + (n : 1) + \cdots + (n : r)$. □

COROLLARY 1b For $r \geq n/2$,

$$\binom{0}{0}\binom{n-1}{r} + \binom{2}{1}\binom{n-3}{r-1} + \binom{4}{2}\binom{n-5}{r-2} + \cdots$$
$$+ \binom{2(n-r-1)}{n-r-1}\binom{2r-n+1}{2r-n+1}$$
$$= \binom{n}{0} + \binom{n}{1} + \binom{n}{2} + \cdots + \binom{n}{n-r-1}.$$

Proof In the theorem, let the distance d between the centers of the two circles be $2(n - r)$. Then the lune is the complement of $O(r, y)$, which is the circle $O(n - r - 1, \grave{y})$. Hence, $|O(n - r - 1, \grave{y})| = (n : 0) + (n : 1) + \cdots + (n : n - r - 1)$. □

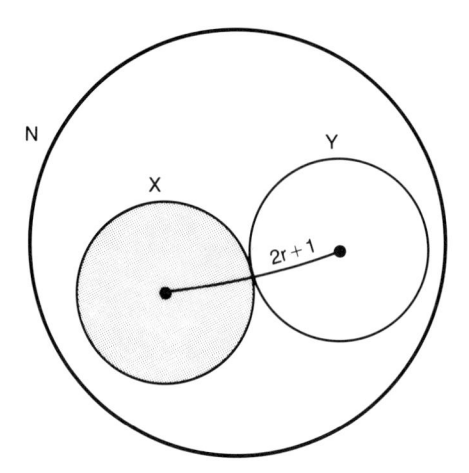

Figure B.2
The lune of two circles that no longer intersect.

Corollaries 1a and 1b state the same fact, by virtue of $(i:j) = (i:i-j)$, but arrive at it through different interpretations.

It is instructive to compare Pascal's triangle with the expression for the area of the lune and to see how the first factor $(0:0)$, $(2:1)$, $(4:2)$, ... goes down vertically starting from the apex of the triangle and the second factor comes up vertically along some column of the triangle. (See figure B.3.) If $r = (n-1)/2$, the second factor too is in the center column, giving the following result:

COROLLARY 2   If m is even,

$$\binom{0}{0}\binom{m}{m/2} + \binom{2}{1}\binom{m-2}{m/2-1} + \binom{4}{2}\binom{m-4}{m/2-2} + \cdots$$
$$+ \binom{m}{m/2}\binom{0}{0} = 2^m.$$

Proof In corollary 1a, let $n = m+1$ and $r = m/2$ and notice that a row of Pascal's triangle adds to a power of 2: $(m+1:0) + \cdots + (m+1:m/2) = 2^{m+1}/2 = 2^m$. Intuitively, the circle $O(m/2, x)$ is exactly half of $\{0, 1\}^{m+1}$. □

Continuous Approximation

Derivation of $g(p, x)$ (Note: In the rest of this appendix, x is a real variable.) We have just seen that the area of a lune is given by the sum of the initial

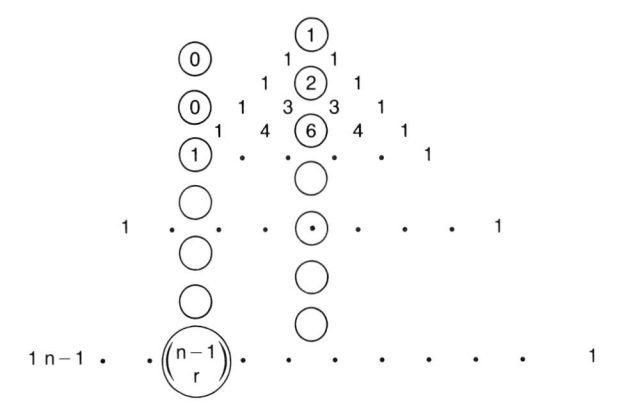

Figure B.3
Pascal's triangle for computing terms of a series.

(first d) terms of the series

$$\binom{0}{0}\binom{n-1}{r} + 0 + \binom{2}{1}\binom{n-3}{r-1} + 0 + \binom{4}{2}\binom{n-5}{r-2} + 0 + \cdots.$$

The terms are generated by two columns of Pascal's triangle. The first factor in each term comes from the center column, starting at the apex, and progresses downward. The second factor starts from $(n - 1 : r)$ and progresses upward in that column. In figure B.3 the entries in the two columns are circled. A continuous approximation of the series is a function that is continuous in the interval $(0, n)$ and the integral of which, from 0 to d, is an estimate of the area of the lune.

We begin by deriving a continuous approximation of Pascal's triangle. This is done by replacing the binomial coefficients $(u : v)$ with their normal approximations, $B(u, v)$. The coefficients of row u have a mean of $u/2$ and a standard deviation of $\sqrt{u}/2$, and their sum is 2^u. The normal approximation of a row is then

$$\binom{u}{v} \cong B(u, v)$$
$$= \frac{2^u}{\sqrt{u/2}} f\left(\frac{v - u/2}{\sqrt{u/2}}\right)$$
$$= \frac{2^{u+1}}{\sqrt{u}} f\left(\frac{2v - u}{\sqrt{u}}\right),$$

where f is the normal density function. For the center column $(u : u/2)$ it equals $(2^{u+1}/\sqrt{u})f(0)$, which evaluates to $2^{u+1/2}/\sqrt{\pi u}$ and which, curiously, is the same as the approximation given by Stirling's factorial formula applied to $u!/(u/2)!^2$. (In general, the normal and Stirling approximations of the binomial coefficients differ.)

The nonzero terms of the series for the lune are products of two binomial coefficients, and they yield

$$\binom{i}{i/2}\binom{n-i-1}{r-i/2}$$

$$\cong \frac{2^{i+1}}{\sqrt{i}} f(0) \frac{2^{n-i}}{\sqrt{n-i-1}} f\left(\frac{2r-n+1}{\sqrt{n-i-1}}\right)$$

$$= \frac{2^{n+1}}{\sqrt{i(n-i-1)}} \frac{1}{2\pi} \exp\left(-\frac{1}{2}\frac{(2r-n+1)^2}{n-i-1}\right)$$

$$\cong 2^n \frac{1}{\pi\sqrt{i(n-i)}} \exp\left(-\frac{1}{2}\frac{(2r-n)^2}{n-i}\right)$$

$$= L(i).$$

The first approximation comes from replacing the binomial coefficients with their normal approximations, and the second from replacing $n-1$ with n everywhere except in the exponent of 2.

To capture the essence of the function $L(i)$, we rewrite $(2r-n)^2$ as $4(n/2-r)^2$ and normalize the difference by dividing it with the standard deviation of the binomial: $n/2 - r = c\sqrt{n}/2$, where $r = r_p$ is the radius of a circle that contains p of N and where $c = c_p$ is the difference $n/2 - r_p$ in standard units. Then $(2r-n)^2 = nc^2$. Substituting this in $L(i)$ and dividing by n in the exponent and under the radical sign gives

$$L(i) = \frac{2^n}{\pi n\sqrt{i/n(1-i/n)}} \exp\left(-\frac{1}{2}\frac{c^2}{1-i/n}\right).$$

The series

$$L(1) + 0 + L(3) + 0 + L(5) + \cdots$$

then approximates the original series, and the sum of the first d terms gives an estimate of the area of the lune.

To get a continuous estimate, average the zero and nonzero terms to

$$L(1)/2 + L(2)/2 + L(3)/2 + L(4)/2 + L(5)/2 + \cdots$$

and evaluate the integral of $L(i)/2$ from 0 to d. To integrate $L(i)/2$, substitute x for i/n, whereby $di = ndx$, giving

$$J(p,d) \cong \int_0^d \frac{L(i)}{2} di$$

$$= 2^n \int_0^{d/n} \frac{1}{2\pi\sqrt{x(1-x)}} \exp\left(-\frac{1}{2}\frac{c_p^2}{1-x}\right) dx.$$

We now have our continuous approximation of the series in normalized form. Let us call it $g(p, x)$:

$$g(p,x) = \frac{1}{2\pi\sqrt{x(1-x)}} \exp\left(-\frac{1}{2}\frac{c_p^2}{1-x}\right) \quad \text{for } 0 < x < 1,$$

where $c = c_p = F^{-1}(p) = (r_p - n/2)/\sqrt{n/4}$ equals the distance, in standard deviations of the distribution of N, from the edge of the circle to the equator of N. The area of the lune of two circles of N is then given by

$$J(p,d) \cong N \int_0^{d/n} g(p,x) dx$$

and, finally, the area of the intersection of two circles is given by

$$I(p,d) \cong N \int_{d/n}^1 g(p,x) dx.$$

The approximation is very good when $0 \ll r \ll n$. In fact, it gives more accurate results than does the exact series when computations are carried out on a computer in single-precision floating-point arithmetic. The normalized intersection function, defined as the portion of the space enclosed by the intersection, is given by

$$i(p,d) \cong \int_d^1 g(p,x) dx, \quad 0 \le p, d \le 1.$$

Here the letter i names a function (earlier it was used for an index variable), and the distance d between the centers of the circles is relative to the number of dimensions n.

Properties of $g(p, x)$ As an interesting aside, consider two special cases. First, the lune of two disjoint circles suggests that the integral of $g(p, x)$ from 0 to 1 is p, which is the fraction of the space N covered by a circle with radius r_p. (This is the continuous counterpart of corollary 1a.) This is easily checked for a circle that covers half the space (for $p = \frac{1}{2}$), because then $c_{0.5} = 0$ and $g(p, x)$ reduces to $1/[2\pi\sqrt{x(1-x)}]$, for which integration gives

$$\frac{1}{2\pi}\int_0^1 \frac{1}{\sqrt{x(1-x)}}\,dx = \frac{1}{2\pi}\arcsin(2x-1)\Big|_0^1$$

$$= \frac{1}{2\pi}\pi$$

$$= \tfrac{1}{2}.$$

This is the continuous counterpart of corollary 2.

In general, as the circles $O(r_p, y)$ and $O(r_p, z)$ separate, the lune $Q(r_p, y, z)$ becomes all of the circle $O(r_p, y)$, which by definition is p of N (assuming that $r < n/2$). This suggests the identity

$$\int_0^1 g(x)\,dx \equiv \int_{-\infty}^{-|c|} f(x)\,dx,$$

where f is the normal density function and $g(x)$ is short for $g(p, x)$. The right side of the identity equals $F(-|c|)$, which is the normal probability at $-|c|$. Written out in full, the identity becomes

$$\frac{1}{2\pi}\int_0^1 \frac{1}{\sqrt{x(1-x)}} \exp\left(-\frac{1}{2}\frac{c^2}{1-x}\right) dx$$

$$\equiv \frac{1}{\sqrt{2\pi}}\int_{-\infty}^{-|c|} \exp(-\tfrac{1}{2}x^2)\,dx.$$

I have not been able to prove this, but it seems to be true on the basis of numeric integration of $g(x)$.

The second special case is the intersection of two orthogonal circles, that is, circles that have their centers at $n/2$ from each other. As n increases, the circles become more and more independent of each another (see "Tendency to Orthogonality" in chapter 1). In the limit, the intersection of $O(r_p, y)$ with $O(r_p, z)$ would then be p of $O(r_p, y)$, or p^2 of N. Since the intersection of two circles with centers at d bits from each other is approximately

$$N\int_{d/n}^1 g(x)\,dx,$$

the proposed identity becomes

$$\int_{1/2}^1 g(x)\,dx \equiv \left(\int_0^1 g(x)\,dx\right)^2,$$

where the right side equals $[F(-|c|)]^2$ according to the first proposed identity. Numeric integration seems to verify it, but here again I do not have a general proof. However, for $p = \tfrac{1}{2}$, it is easily seen to be true.

Appendix C
The Fidelity of Sparse Distributed Memory

Fidelity is a measure of how well a previously written word can be read. More precisely, fidelity of memory is defined here as the probability that a bit of a word written at ξ (i.e., written with the address ξ) is recovered by reading at x. The closer the reading address x is to the writing address ξ, the higher the fidelity. As the distance between the two addresses increases, fidelity falls rapidly to $\frac{1}{2}$, which corresponds to random noise.

The following parameters of distributed storage will be used in this appendix:

- N' the hard locations (a random sample of N), and also their number
- p a probability ($0 \leq p \leq 1$)
- r_p the radius of a circle that covers p of N (and of N'): $|O(r_p, y)| = pN$, and since $O'(r_p, y) = O(r_p, y) \cap N'$, $|O'(r_p, y)| \cong pN'$ ($y \in N$)
- T the age of memory, that is, the number of write operations performed so far (each write operation stores a datum in approximately pN' locations).

Let the data stored in memory be the (multi)set of T address–datum pairs $\langle \xi_t, \eta_t \rangle$, where $t = 0, 1, 2, \ldots, T - 1$. The data element $\langle \xi, \eta \rangle$ is stored by writing the word η at ξ. That means writing it *in*, or adding it to the contents of, each hard location accessible from ξ—that is, in the locations $O'(r_p, \xi)$. Then reading at x means pooling the contents of the locations accessible from x, $O'(r_p, x)$, and taking the average of the pooled data.

For brevity of notation, access circles will be written without their radii. For example, $O'(x)$ will mean $O'(r_p, x)$. Further, I'_t will stand for the size of the access overlap (intersection) of the read circle located at x with the tth write circle located at ξ_t:

$$I'_t = |O'(x) \cap O'(\xi_t)|.$$

Then reading at x retrieves I'_t copies of the word η_t that was written at ξ_t ($t = 0, 1, \ldots, T - 1$).

The rest of this appendix is concerned with just one coordinate of the stored data—the contents of the ith bit locations—as that is all that is needed to compute fidelity. To simplify the mathematics, we will assume that writing happens as follows: If the ith bit of a word written in a bit location is 0, subtract 1 from the contents of the bit location; if it is 1, add 1 to the contents of the bit location. For the stored word η_t, denote this ith bit increment by i_t ($= -1, 1$). Let I' stand for the pooled ith bit sum obtained by reading at x,

$$I' = \sum_{t=0}^{T-1} I'_t i_t.$$

The ith bit of the word at x, $W_i(x)$, is then interpreted as being 1 if I' exceeds the mean value $\mathrm{E}\{I'\}$ and as 0 otherwise.

In deriving an expression for fidelity, our biggest task will be measuring the random variation in the pooled data, or the variance of I'. Comparing the weight I'_t of the word η_t in the pooled data with this variation then gives us the fidelity at x for the word η_t.

In estimating the variance of I', notice first that, for any given past $\langle \xi_t, \eta_t \rangle$ ($t = 0, 1, \ldots, T-1$), the written data i_t are fixed, so that the variance of the pooled sum I' is due to the variation in the size of the overlap I'_t of the read and write circles. Second, for the large values of n and the small values of p that concern us here, the variables I'_t can be considered independent. Then the variance of the sum I' is the sum of the variances of T access overlaps:

$$\mathrm{Var}\{I'\} = T\,\mathrm{Var}\{I'_t i_t\} \quad \text{(variance of a sum of } T \text{ independent,}$$
$$\text{equally distributed variables)}$$
$$= T\,\mathrm{Var}\{i_t^2 I'_t\} \quad \text{(variance of a constant times a variable)}$$
$$= T\,\mathrm{Var}\{I'_t\} \quad \text{(since } i_t = -1, 1\text{).}$$

We are left with evaluating $\mathrm{Var}\{I'_t\}$, the variation in the intersection $|O'(x) \cap O'(\xi_t)|$ of two access circles of N'. It has two independent components: variation in the expected size of the intersection (variation in $|O(x) \cap O(\xi_t)|$) and variation in the actual number of locations $|O'(x) \cap O'(\xi_t)|$ given $|O(x) \cap O(\xi_t)|$. Let I_t be the expected size of the intersection,

$$I_t = \mathrm{E}\{I'_t\}$$
$$= \mathrm{E}\{|O'(x) \cap O'(\xi_t)|\}$$
$$= (N'/N)|O(x) \cap O(\xi_t)|$$

and let e_t be deviation of I'_t from it, and write

$$I'_t = I_t + e_t.$$

To use this breakdown of I'_t, we will make two simplifying assumptions: that I_t is a linear function of the distance between the two circles, and that the variation of e_t is constant. These assumptions hold well for the bulk of the distribution of I'_t when n is large and p is small, as they are here. We can then write the variance as

$$\text{Var}\{I'_t\} = \text{Var}\{I_t\} + \text{Var}\{e_t\}$$

and use a linear approximation of the intersection function to estimate it—the linear function being the tangent of the intersection function at $n/2$, that is, when the distance between the two circles (between their centers) is the mean distance in N.

To estimate the variation in the intersection I_t, let $I(d)$ stand for the expected size of the intersection as a function of the distance between the circles (see figure 1.2), let H stand for the slope of this function at $n/2$, and let $\text{Var}\{d\}$ stand for the variance of distance in N. Then

$$\text{Var}\{I_t\} \cong H^2 \text{Var}\{d\} = H^2(n/4) = \frac{(h_p N')^2}{4n},$$

where h_p is the slope of the normalized $I(d)$ at $\frac{1}{2}$. (The domain and the range of a normalized $I(d)$ are $[0, 1]$, and so $H = (N'/n)h$.) An expression for the normalized $I(d)$ is derived in appendix B, and its slope at $\frac{1}{2}$ is

$$h_p = -g(p, \tfrac{1}{2}) = \frac{1}{x}\exp(-c_p)^2,$$

where $c_p = F^{-1}(p)$. If each access circle covers $1/1{,}000$ of the space N ($p = 0.001$), then $c = -3.09$ and $h = -0.000023$.

We will now estimate the variation $\text{Var}\{e_t\}$ around the expected value of the intersection—that is, the variation in the number of hard locations falling in $O(x) \cap O(\xi_t)$. Since N' is a random sample of N and $N' \gg I_t$, the number of locations in $O(x) \cap O(\xi_t)$ is approximately Poisson distributed with the parameter I_t and so has variance I_t. For the mean distance in N the intersection is $p^2 N'$, so that

$$\text{Var}\{e_t\} \cong p^2 N'.$$

Collecting the results yields

$$\text{Var}\{I'\} \cong T \text{Var}\{I'_t\}$$
$$\cong T(\text{Var}\{I_t\} + \text{Var}\{e_t\})$$
$$\cong T\left(\frac{(hN')^2}{4n} + p^2 N'\right)$$
$$= \left(\frac{h^2 N'}{4n} + p^2\right) N' T.$$

To make the dominant part of the expression in parentheses stand out, we will write the above as

$$\text{Var}\{I'\} \cong \left(1 + \frac{h^2 N'}{4p^2 n}\right) p^2 N' T.$$

For the sample memory (i.e., $n = 1{,}000$, $N' = 1{,}000{,}000$, $p = 0.001$), we get $h = -0.000023$, and the expression in the parentheses is $(1 + 0.13)$. Hence, the term e_t contributes most (88 percent) of the variation. For parameter values like these we can then write

$$\text{Var}\{I'\} \cong p^2 N' T.$$

To get an expression for the signal-to-noise ratio for the word η_t at x, divide the weight I'_t in the pooled data I' by the standard deviation $\text{Std}\{I'\}$. The weight, as a function of the distance d between the write and the read addresses, is $i(p, d/n)N'$, where i is the normalized intersection function of appendex B. For the signal-to-noise ratio we then get

$$R(p, N', T, d) \cong \frac{i(p, d/n) N'}{[(1 + h^2 N'/4p^2 n) p^2 N' T]^{1/2}}$$

$$= \frac{i(p, d/n)}{p} \left(\frac{N'}{(1 + h^2 N'/4p^2 n) T}\right)^{1/2}.$$

The maximum signal-to-noise ratio is obtained by reading at the write address. Then $d = 0$, the intersection $i(p, d/n) = p$, and the fraction $i(p, d/n)/p$ equals 1. If we now approximate the multiplier of T with 1, as discussed above, we get

$$R_{max} \cong \sqrt{N'/T},$$

where N' is the number of hard locations and T is the size of the data set stored in memory (number of write operations, age). Notice that this maximum is independent of p for small p.

Finally, the normal distribution function gives the fidelity as

$$P(p, N', T, d) = F(R(p, N', T, d)).$$

For the maximum fidelity we have

$$P_{max} \cong F(\sqrt{N'/T}),$$

which, again, is independent of p, and which is convenient for estimating memory capacity (see chapter 7). For example, if $N' = 1{,}000{,}000$ and $T = 10{,}000$, the maximum fidelity equals $F(10)$, which equals $1 - 0.76 \cdot 10^{-23}$.

Appendix D
The Distance between Two Read Chains

Two words read at two random points (reading addresses) are nearly independent of each other. However, if the two points are close to each other, the read circles overlap considerably, so that the words retrieved ought to be similar to each other. Exactly how similar is the subject of this appendix. The answer is most easily seen with reference to the best-match problem.

The data set X is stored in memory by writing each word ξ at ξ. Reading at u then pools the data of the locations in the access circle $O'(u)$. Likewise, reading at v pools the locations $O'(v)$. What, then, is the distance between the two words $W(u)$ and $W(v)$ computed from the two sets of pooled data?

To answer the question, it suffices to look at just one bit of the two words read from memory. The ith bit is obtained by comparing the ith bit sum of the pooled data with the mean sum. If the ith bit sums in the two data were independent of each another, the ith bits of $W(u)$ and $W(v)$ would also be independent, as would be the words $W(u)$ and $W(v)$ (and the distance between them would be approximately $n/2$). However, when the read circles $O'(u)$ and $O'(v)$ overlap, the two bit sums are correlated, and the two read words are not independent.

We will first find the correlation between the two ith bit sums. From it we will determine the probability that the bit sums fall on different sides of the mean, meaning that the ith bits of $W(u)$ and $W(v)$ will differ. That probability gives the distance between the two words.

Assume, first, that no word has been written near the two addresses u and v at which the memory is read. This would be the usual case if one reading address were taken at random and the other were taken close to it, also at random. The correlation R between the ith bit sums can then be estimated as follows: The ith bit sum at u is the sum of the ith bit locations accessible from u; it is the sum of $|O'(u)|$ (nearly) independent, equally distributed random variables. Likewise, the ith bit sum at v is the sum of $|O'(v)|$ independent, equally distributed random variables. The two sums have $|O'(u) \cap O'(v)|$ variables in common, and therefore the correlation between the sums is given by

$$R \cong \frac{|O'(u) \cap O'(v)|}{\sqrt{|O'(u)| \cdot |O'(v)|}}.$$

Using the expected numbers of locations for the actual numbers gives

$$R \cong \frac{|O(u) \cap O(v)|}{|O(u)|}$$

$$\cong \frac{i(p, d(u, v)/n)}{p},$$

where $i(p, d)$ is the normalized intersection function of appendix B. Table 1.3 can be read as a tabulation of R.

We will next find the probability that the ith bits of $W(u)$ and $W(v)$ differ. Call the two bit sums U and V, respectively. As they are sums of (nearly) independent, equally distributed random variables, their joint distribution is approximately binomial, with correlation coefficient R. The ith bits differ if U is above the mean sum and V below, or vice versa. That probability can be obtained by integrating the standardized binormal distribution $f(R, x, y)$ over the second and fourth quadrants. (Note: In this appendix, x and y are real variables.) By the symmetry of the normal function $f(R, x, y)$, the probability is twice the integral over, say, the fourth quadrant:

$$\Pr\{(W_i(u) \neq W_i(v)\} \cong 2 \int_0^{-\infty} \int_0^{\infty} f(R, x, y) \, dx \, dy.$$

With a simple geometric argument, we will establish $\frac{1}{4} - \arcsin R/(2\pi)$ as the value of the double integral. Therefore, the probability that the ith bits of $W(u)$ and $W(v)$ differ is approximately

$$\frac{1}{2} - \frac{\arcsin R}{\pi}.$$

The contour lines of the standardized binormal distribution with correlation 0, $f(0, x, y) = $ constant, are circles with centers at the origin, and those of $f(R, x, y)$ are ellipses with the 45° lines $y = x$ and $y = -x$ as their major and minor axes. ($y = x$ is the major axis if R is positive.) Figure D.1 shows the contour circle of $f(0, x, y)$ with radius 1 (on the left) and its transform when the correlation R is positive (on the right). The double integral is over the shaded area on the right, which is a transform of the shaded area on the left. The corresponding probability (the value of the double integral) is then proportional to the angle Q of the shaded area on the left, the full plane (360°) having probability 1.

The angle Q is found by finding first the x at which the ellipse on the

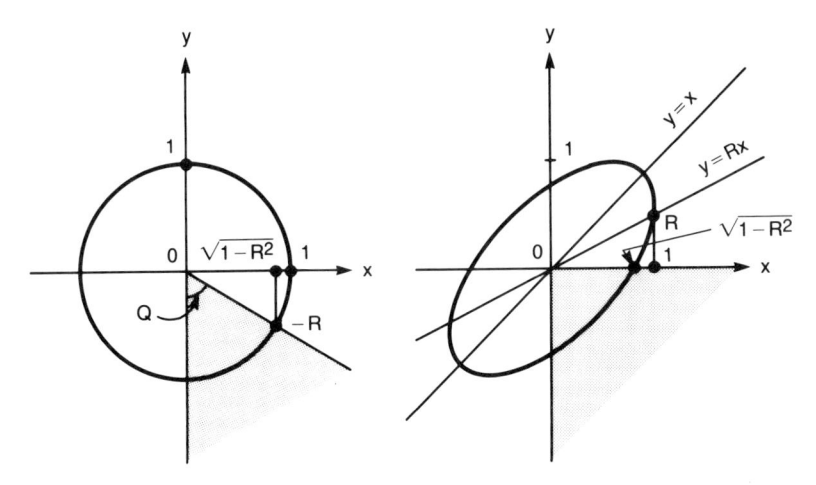

Figure D.1
Standardized binormal distributions with correlations 0 and R ($R > 0$). The probabilities of the two shaded areas are equal.

right intersects the x axis. Since $f(R, x, y)$ is binormal, the variance of y can be decomposed as

$$\text{Var}(y) = R^2 \text{Var}(x) + \text{Var}(y|x).$$

Because $\text{Var}(x) = \text{Var}(y) = 1$, this becomes

$$1 = R^2 + \text{Var}(y|x),$$

and because the conditional distribution of $y - x$ given x is independent of x, we get

$$\text{Var}(y|x = 0) = 1 - R^2.$$

The standard deviation is then

$$\text{Std}(y|x = 0) = \sqrt{1 - R^2},$$

which is where the ellipse intersects the y axis. By the symmetry of the function $f(R, x, y)$ with respect to x and y, $\sqrt{1 - R^2}$ is also where the ellipse intersects the x axis. The complement of the angle Q in the left diagram of figure D.1 is then arcsin R, and the probability of the shaded area is $\frac{1}{4} -$ arcsin $R/2\pi$. Twice that is the probability that the ith bits of $W(u)$ and $W(v)$ differ, as stated above.

We now have our result when the two reading addresses are far from any previously written address. If the two are d bits apart, the words read are $(\frac{1}{2} -$ arcsin $R/\pi)n$ bits apart, on the average, where $R = i(p, d/n)/p$. Table 7.3 shows the distance for $n = 1,000$ and $p = 0.001$. Even a one-bit difference in the initial reading address makes a big difference in what is read, and after one or two more read operations the chains are independent.

When the two reading addresses u and v are well within the critical distance of a previously written address ξ, the two read chains will converge to ξ. But if the "pull" of ξ is factored out, the chains diverge. For example, if in reading from the sample memory the addresses u and v are just one bit apart but are 130 bits away from the nearest write address, ξ, the read words $W(u)$ and $W(v)$ will each be about 33 bits from ξ according to table 7.2. Therefore they cannot be 132 bits from each other, as would be suggested by table 7.3, but they would be much farther from each other than the original distance of one bit—possibly 20 bits. The proof of this is similar to the one above, involving integration over the second and fourth quadrants, except that the center of the binomial distribution would not be at the origin.

Appendix E
Commonly Used Symbols

Symbol	As in	Description
`	`x	complement (opposite) of a point
| |	$\|x\|$	norm of a vector (number of ones)
| |	$\|X\|$	number of elements in a set
$\oplus$	$x \oplus y$	'exclusive or'
:	$x:y:z$	between: "y is between x and z"
$\perp$	$x \perp y$	perpendicular, orthogonal to
(:)	$(i:j)$	binomial coefficient $\dfrac{i!}{j!(i-j)!}$, same as $\binom{i}{j}$
\	$A \backslash B$	set difference $A \cap \bar{B}$
'	x'	nearest N'-neighbor of x (a hard location)
:=	$X := X \cup Y$	assignment
$\uplus$	$A \uplus B$	multiunion (of multisets)
[ ]	$[A, A, B]$	multiset
$\square$		end of proof
0		the number zero, and also the zero-vector $(0, 0, \ldots, 0)$
a		binary address ($a \in N$)
a_i		ith coordinate of address
c		threshold
c_p		$F^{-1}(p)$
d		distance, usually in bits
$d(x, y)$		distance between x and y
$D(t)$		k-fold pooled data at time t
$D(x)$		pooled data at x
$D_j(x)$		pooled data at x from jth fold
$E\{x\}$		expectation of x (x scalar)
$f(\cdots)$		normal density function
$F(\cdots)$		normal distribution function
$g(p, x)$		differential of the normalized lune of two circles ($0 \leq x \leq 1$)
$g(x)$		short for $g(p, x)$

Appendix E

Symbol	Description
h	slope of the access-overlap function at $\frac{1}{2}$, $i'(\frac{1}{2})$
$H(\cdots)$	$F^{-1}(\cdots)$ (in computing capacity of memory)
$i(p, x)$	area of the intersection of two circles relative to N ($0 \leq x \leq 1$)
$i(x)$	short for $i(p, x)$
$I(p, d)$	area of the intersection of two circles ($0 \leq d \leq n$)
$I(d)$	short for $I(p, d)$
$I'(x, y)$	access overlap of two circles: $I'(x, y) = O'(x) \cap O'(y)$
iff	if and only if
$J(p, d)$	area of lune as a function of distance between circles
$J(d)$	short for $J(p, d)$
$L(i)$	approximation of lune increment
n	number of dimensions
N	$\{0, 1\}^n$, and also 2^n
$N(d)$	distribution of distance in N
N'	(multi)set of hard locations (elements of N' are in N), and also number of hard locations
$N'(d)$	distribution of distance to nearest location in N'
N'_j	hard locations of the jth fold, and also their number
$O(r, x)$	circle with radius r and center x: $O(r, x) = \{y \mid x, y \in N \ \& \ d(x, y) \leq r\}$
$O(x)$	short for $O(r, x)$
$O'(r, x)$	the hard locations in $O(r, x)$: $O'(r, x) = O(r, x) \cap N'$ $= \{y \mid y \in N' \ \& \ x \in N \ \& \ d(x, y) \leq r\}$
$O'(x)$	short for $O'(r, x)$
p	probability: $0 \leq p \leq 1$
P	fidelity: $P = F(R)$
$P(d)$	fidelity at distance d
$\Pr\{A\}$	probability of event A
$\Pr\{A \mid B\}$	probability of A given B
$Q(r, x, y)$	lune: $Q(r, x, y) = O(r, x) \setminus O(r, y)$
r	radius, in bits
r_p	radius, in bits, of a circle that includes p of N: $\lvert O(r_p, x) \rvert / N = p$
R	signal-to-noise ratio
s	minimum weighted sum: the sum of negative coefficients
S	maximum weighted sum: the sum of positive coefficients
$\mathrm{Std}\{x\}$	standard deviation of x (x scalar)
t	point of time
T	age of memory (number of write operations)
$\mathrm{Var}\{x\}$	variance of x (x scalar)
w_i	ith input weight of a linear threshold function

Commonly Used Symbols

Symbol	Description
$W(t)$	word read at time t
$W(x)$	word at x
X	data set stored in memory
$X(T)$	time series $\langle \xi_0, \ldots, \xi_t, \ldots, \xi_{T-1} \rangle$ ($\xi_t \in N$)
$\langle \xi_{t-1}, \xi_t \rangle$	(first-order) transition occurring in $X(T)$
$\langle \xi_{t-j}, \xi_t \rangle$	j-step transition occurring in $X(T)$
ξ, η, ζ	(without or with subscripts): words of a data set or sequence stored in memory; they become addresses used in writing into memory (centers of write circles), and words written into memory
z	test word
ζ	target word (a word of the stored data set)

Bibliography

Albus, J. S. 1971. A theory of cerebellar functions. *Mathematical Biosciences* 10(1/2):25–61.
Albus, J. S. 1975. A new approach to manipulator control: The cerebellar model articulation controller (CMAC). *American Society of Mechanical Engineers, Transactions G (Journal of Dynamic Systems, Measurement, and Control)* 97(3):220–227.
Albus, J. S. 1981. *Brains, Behavior, and Robotics*. Peterborough, N.H.: Byte Books.
Aleksander, I. 1970. Some psychological properties of digital learning nets. *International Journal of Man-Machine Studies* 2:189–212.
Aleksander, I., and T. J. Stonham. 1979. Guide to pattern recognition using random-access memories. *IEE Journal on Computers and Digital Techniques* 2(1):29–40.
Anderson, J. A. 1968. A memory storage module utilizing spatial correlation functions. *Kybernetik* 5(3):113–119.
Anderson, J. A. 1970. Two models for memory organization using interacting traces. *Mathematical Biosciences* 8:137–160.
Anderson, J. A. 1977. Neural models with cognitive implications. In D. LaBerge and S. J. Samuels (eds.), *Basic Processes in Reading: Perception and Comprehension* (Hillsdale, N.J.: Erlbaum).
Anderson, J. A. 1983. Cognitive and psychological computation with neural models. *IEEE Transactions on Systems, Man, and Cybernetics* 13(5):799–815.
Anderson, J. A. 1986. Cognitive capabilities of a parallel system. In E. Bienenstock, F. Fogelman Soulié, and G. Weisbuch (eds.), *Disordered Systems and Biological Organization* (NATO ASI Series F, vol. 20) (Berlin: Springer-Verlag).
Anderson, J. A., and G. E. Hinton. 1981. Models of information processing in the brain. In G. E. Hinton and J. A. Anderson (eds.), *Parallel Models of Associative Memory* (Hillsdale, N.J.: Erlbaum).
Anderson, J. A., and G. L. Murphy. 1986. Psychological concepts in a parallel system. *Physica* 22D:318–336.
Baum, E. B., J. Moody, and F. Wilczek. 1986. Internal Representations for Associative Memory. Report NSF-ITP-86-138, Institute for Theoretical Physics, University of California, Santa Barbara.
Block, H. D. 1970. Review of *Perceptrons: An Introduction to Computational Geometry*. *Information and Control* 17:501–522.
Blumenthal, L. M., and K. Menger. 1970. *Studies in Geometry*. San Francisco: Freeman.
Bower, G. 1967. A multicomponent theory of the memory trace. *Psychology of Learning and Motivation* 1:229–325. Reprinted in G. Bower (ed.), *Human Memory: Basic Processes* (New York: Academic, 1977).
Brindley, G. S. 1969. Nerve net models of plausible size that perform many simple learning tasks. *Proceedings of the Royal Society of London* B 174:173–191.
Eccles, J. C. 1975. Under the spell of the synapse. In F. G. Worden, J. P. Swazey, and G. Adelman (eds.), *The Neurosciences: Paths of Discovery* (Cambridge, Mass.: MIT Press).

Eccles, J. C., M. Ito, and J. Szentagothai. 1967. *The Cerebellum as a Neuronal Machine.* Berlin: Springer-Verlag.
Feldman, J. A., and D. H. Ballard. 1982. Connectionist models and their properties. *Cognitive Science* 6(3): 205–254.
Feller, W. 1957. *An Introduction to Probability Theory and Its Applications,* second edition, volume 1. New York: Wiley.
Foster, C. F. 1976. *Content Addressable Parallel Processors.* New York: Van Nostrand Reinhold.
Fredkin, E. 1960. Trie memory. *Communications of the ACM* 3: 490–499.
Grossberg, S. 1980. How does a brain build a cognitive code? *Psychological Review* 87: 1–51. Reprinted in Grossberg 1983.
Grossberg, S. 1983. *Studies of Mind and Brain* (Boston Studies in the Philosophy of Science, volume 70). Boston: Reidel.
Hebb, D. O. 1949. *Organization of Behavior: A Neuropsychological Theory.* New York: Wiley.
Hinton, G. E., T. J. Sejnowski, and D. H. Ackley. 1984. Boltzmann Machines: Constraint Satisfaction Networks that Learn. Report CMU-CS-84-119, Department of Computer Science, Carnegie-Mellon University.
Hofstadter, D. R. 1985. *Metamagical Themas.* New York: Basic Books.
Holland, J. H. 1986. Escaping brittleness: The possibilities of general-purpose learning algorithms applied to parallel rule-based systems. In R. S. Michalski, J. G. Carbonell, and T. M. Mitchell (eds.), *Machine Learning: An Artificial Intelligence Approach,* volume 2 (Los Altos, Calif.: Kaufmann).
Holland, J. H., K. J. Holyoak, R. E. Nisbett, and P. R. Thagard. 1986. *Induction: Processes of Inference, Learning, and Discovery.* Cambridge, Mass.: MIT Press.
Hopfield, J. J. 1982. Neural networks and physical systems with emergent collective computational abilities. *Proceedings of the National Academy of Sciences (Biophysics)* 79(8): 2554–2558.
Ito, M. 1982. Mechanisms of motor learning. In S. Amari and M. A. Arbib (eds.), *Competition and Cooperation in Neural Nets* (Lecture Notes in Biomathematics, volume 45) (Berlin: Springer-Verlag).
Kanerva, P. 1984. Self-Propagating Search: A Unified Theory of Memory. Report CSLI-84-7, Center for the Study of Language and Information, Stanford University.
Kanerva, P. 1986. Parallel structures in human and computer memory. In J. S. Denker (ed.), *Neural Networks for Computing* (AIP Conference Proceedings, volume 151) (New York: American Institute of Physics).
Knuth, D. E. 1981. *Seminumerical Algorithms: The Art of Computer Programming,* second edition, volume 2. Reading, Mass.: Addison-Wesley.
Kohonen, T. 1972. Correlation matrix memories. *IEEE Transactions on Computers* C 21(4): 353–359.
Kohonen, T. 1977. *Associative Memory: A System-Theoretic Approach.* New York: Springer-Verlag.
Kohonen, T. 1984. *Self-Organization and Associative Memory,* second edition. New York: Springer-Verlag.
Llinás, R. R. 1975. The cortex of the cerebellum. *Scientific American* 232(1): 56–71.
Loftus, E. F. 1979. *Eyewitness Testimony.* Cambridge, Mass.: Harvard University Press.
Marr, D. 1969. A theory of cerebellar cortex. *Journal of Physiology* 202: 437–470.
Marr, D. 1970. A theory for cerebral neocortex. *Proceedings of the Royal Society of London* B 176: 161–234.
Marr, D. 1971. Simple memory: A theory for archicortex. *Philosophical Transactions of the Royal Society of London* B 262: 23–81.
McClelland, J. L., and D. E. Rumelhart, eds. 1986. *Parallel Distributed Processing: Explorations in the Microstructure of Cognition,* volume 2. Cambridge, Mass.: MIT Press. (For volume 1 see Rumelhart and McClelland 1986.)

McCulloch, W. S., and W. Pitts. 1943. A logical calculus of the ideas immanent in nervous activity. *Bulletin of Mathematical Biophysics* 5:115–133.

Minsky, M. 1954. Theory of Neural-Analog Reinforcement Systems and Its Application to the Brain-Model Problem. Doctoral dissertation, Princeton University (University Microfilms, no. 9438).

Minsky, M., and S. Papert. 1969. *Perceptrons: An Introduction to Computational Geometry.* Cambridge, Mass.: MIT Press.

Nilsson, N. J. 1965. *Learning Machines: Foundations of Trainable Pattern-Classification Systems.* New York: McGraw-Hill.

Palay, S. L., and V. Chan-Palay. 1974. *Cerebellar Cortex: Cytology and Organization.* New York: Springer-Verlag.

Pylyshyn, Z. W., ed. 1987. *The Robot's Dilemma: The Frame Problem of Artificial Intelligence.* Norwood, N. J.: Ablex.

Rosenblatt, F. 1958. The Perceptron: A Theory of Statistical Separability in Cognitive Systems. Project PARA report VG-1196-6-1, Cornell Aeronautical Laboratory, Buffalo, N.Y.

Rosenblatt, F. 1962. *Principles of Neurodynamics.* Washington, D.C.: Spartan.

Rumelhart, D. E., G. E. Hinton, and R. J. Williams. 1986. Learning internal representations by error propagation. In Rumelhart and McClelland 1986.

Rumelhart, D. E., and J. L. McClelland, eds. 1986. *Parallel Distributed Processing: Explorations in the Microstructure of Cognition,* volume 1. Cambridge, Mass.: MIT Press. (For volume 2 see McClelland and Rumelhart 1986.)

Schank, R. C. 1982. *Dynamic Memory.* Cambridge University Press.

Sejnowski, T. J., and C. R. Rosenberg. 1987. Parallel networks that learn to pronounce English text. *Complex Systems* 1(1):145–168.

Thurber, K. J. 1976. *Large Scale Computer Architecture: Parallel and Associative Processors.* Rochelle Park, N.J.: Hayden.

von Neumann, J. 1951. The general and logical theory of automata. In L. A. Jeffress (ed.), *Cerebral Mechanisms in Behavior: The Hixon Symposium* (New York: Wiley). Reprinted in A. H. Taub (ed.), *John von Neumann: Collected Works,* volume 5 (New York: Pergamon, 1963).

von Neumann, J. 1952. Probabilistic Logics and the Synthesis of Reliable Organisms from Unreliable Components. Lecture, California Institute of Technology. Reprinted in C. E. Shannon and J. McCarthy (eds.), *Automata Studies* (Princeton University Press, 1965), and in A. H. Taub (ed.), *John von Neumann: Collected Works,* volume 5 (New York: Pergamon, 1963).

von Neumann, J. 1958. *The Computer and the Brain.* New Haven: Yale University Press.

Widrow, B. 1962. Generalization and information storage in networks of ADALINE "neurons." In M. C. Yovits, G. T. Jacobi, and G. O. Goldstein (eds.), *Self-Organizing Systems 1962* (Washington, D.C.: Spartan).

Willshaw, D. 1981. Holography, associative memory, and inductive generalization. In G. E. Hinton and J. A. Anderson (eds.), *Parallel Models of Associative Memory* (Hillsdale, N.J.: Erlbaum).

Willshaw, D. J., and H. C. Longuet-Higgins. 1970. Associative memory models. *Machine Intelligence* 5:351–359.

Index

Abstraction, 98, 117
Access circle, 62
Access overlap, 62–64, 67
Access radius, 62
Ackley, D. H., 11
Action
  as interpretation, 114–115
  observable, 103
  side effects of, 113
Action component, 115
Action sequences
  completion of, 105–106
  desirable and undesirable, 107, 109
  generation of, 107–108
Address decoder, 4, 14, 29–32
Address-decoder neuron, 43, 50, 54, 89
Address decoding, 29–32, 87
  as parallel computing, 52
Address of a neuron, 43
Address register, 30
Address space, 30. *See also* Memory space
  vastness of, 53
Addressing
  fixed, 3, 41, 43
  of memory, 30
Albus, James, 9, 11, 117
Aleksander, I., 11
Anderson, James A., 11, 117
Artificial intelligence, traditional, 115, 118
Associative memory, 34
Associative-strength models of memory, 81
Attraction, by write addresses, 98
Autonomous learning system, 97–120
Average word, 88

Back-propagation network, 11
Backtracking search, 109
Ballard, D. H., 11

Basket cell, 91–93
Baum, E. B., 11
Best match
  convergence to, 68
  vs. good match, 51
Best-Match Machine, 50–52, 56, 61, 66
Best-match problem, 49–50, 65–66, 139
Betweenness, 16, 17
Binomial distribution, 18
Bit counter, overflow of, 75
Bit location, 89
  construction of, 90
Bit sum, 88
  variance of, 83
Block, H, D., 9
Blumenthal, L. M., 15
Boolean functions, realized with neurons, 8
Bower, G., 23
Brain damage, 77
Brindley, G. S., 9
Bucket-brigade algorithm, 109

Cerebellum, 4, 9–11, 91–93
  granular layer of, 91
  molecular layer of, 91
  as random-access memory, 90–93
Chan-Palay, V., 91
Circle, 17–18
  access, 62
  area of, 21–22
  distribution of, 21–23
Codon cell, 9–10
Codon representation, 10
Common sense, 113
Complement of a point, 15, 17
Computer, and brain, 6, 9, 29
Conditioning classical (Pavlovian), 99, 110–111

Index

Content-addressable memory, 33–34, 53, 79
Contents of a location, 63
Convergence, 10, 72, 80
  to best match, 68
  chance, 72–73
  and divergence, 142
  rate of, 72–73
  to a sequence, 82
Correction pattern, 102

Data
  at an address, 64
  multifold, 84
  pooled, 64, 67
de Bruijn, N. G., 27
Delay, 84, 86, 89
Difference pattern, 16–17
Distance, 16–17
  between locations, 54
  between read chains, 139–142
  critical, 72, 77
  hamming, 16–17, 49
  indifference, 16
  to a location, 54
  weighted, 46
Divergence, 69–70, 72
  rate of, 72–73

Eccles, J. C., 35, 91
Encoding problem, 116–117
Equator, 18–19
Expectation, 99. See also Predicting
Experience, 113
  as sequence, 80
  subjective, 100–101, 114–115

Feldman, J. A., 11
Feller, W., 124
Fiber
  climbing, 10, 91–94
  mossy, 9, 91–94
  parallel, 10–11
Fidelity, 71, 135–138
First-order machine, 84
First-order stochastic process, 84
Focus, 101–103, 114–115
Forgetting, 76–77
Foster, C. F., 33
Frame problem, 112, 117
Fredkin, E., 12
Function counter, 109

Generalization. See Abstraction
Golgi cell, 91–93
"Grandmother" cell, 11
Granule cell, 9, 91–95
Grossberg, S., 11, 117

Hard location, 54, 62
  construction of, 88
  neuron as, 88–90
Hash coding, 12, 51
Hebb, D. O., 8
Hebb's cell-assembly theory, 9
Hidden layer, 11
Higher-order machine, 84
Hinton, G. E., 11
Hofstadter, D. R., 118
Holland, J. H., 109
Holyoak, K. J., 109
Hopfield, J. J., 11
Hyperplane, 38, 40

Imitation, as a means to learning, 111–112
Indifferent points, 16
Indifferent states, 107
Individual, as interpreter of world or world model, 115
Inherently good and bad states, 107, 111
Input and output lines, matched pairs of, 90
Input coefficient, 35, 39
Interference, proactive and retroactive, 3
Internal model of the world
  action in, 103–106
  nature of, 99–100
  updating of, 101–103, 106
Interpretation
  in action, 114–115
  in subjective experience, 114–115
Intersection of two circles, 23–25, 125–134
  continuous approximation of, 130–134
Ito, M., 11, 91

Knowing that one knows, 2, 58, 76
Knuth, D. E., 26
Kohonen, T., 11

Learning
  to act, 106–112
  from experience, 99
  initial conditions for, 107–108
  social, 110, 115

speed of, 110
supervised, 99, 110–111
Learning system, autonomous, 97–120
Learning theory, mathematical, 81, 110
Linear threshold function, 36
Linearly separable sets, 38–40
Linked list, 12
List, 26
Llinás, R. R., 91, 92
Loftus, E. F., 100
Longuet-Higgins, H. C., 11
Low-level representation, importance of, 117–118
Lune increment, 126–129, 132
Lune of two circles, 125–134

Markov chain, 84
Markov process, 81
Marr, David, 9–11, 81, 91
McClelland, J. L., 11
McCulloch, W. S., 8, 35
Meaning, 114
Meaningful events and experiences, 111–112
Memory
  accessing of, as computing, 51–52
  addressing of, 30
  associative, 34
  associative-strength models of, 81
  capacity of, 74–76
  content-addressable, 33–34, 53, 79
  distributed, 61–77
  failure-driven, 111
  localized models of, 11
  multifold, 84
  multistep, 84
  random-access, 30–32, 61, 79
  sample, 55–56, 62, 65
  sequential-access, 30, 32
Memory item, 1, 15, 23–26
Memory record, 1, 100
Memory space, 14–15, 23–26. *See also* Semantic space
  distribution of, 18–20
Mendel's theory of heredity, 7
Menger, K., 15
Minsky, M., 8, 38, 49
Moody, J., 11
Motor component, 103–106
Multiset, 26
Multiunion, 27
Murphy, G. L., 117

Nearest hard location, 54–56
  median distance to, 56
Nearest-neighbor method, 46, 56–59, 76
Neuron
  address of, 43
  as address decoder (*see* Address-decoder neuron)
  as storage location, 88–90
Neuron memory, robustness of, 48, 51, 77
Neuron model, 35
Nilsson, N. J., 39
Nisbett, R. E., 109
Noise, 71
Norm, 16, 17
Normal distribution, 18

Objects and individuals, formation of, 98–99, 116
Origin, 15
Orthogonal, 16,17
Orthogonality, tendency to, 19

Palay, S. L., 91
Papert, S., 38, 49
Parallel computing, 52, 118
  by address decoders, 32
Parallel processing, 11
Pascal's triangle, and its normal approximation, 130–132
Pattern classification, 38
Pattern recognition, 45, 98
Pavlovian learning. *See* Conditioning
Perceptron, 9, 37–41
Perceptron-convergence learning, 38–40, 48
  implicit assumptions in, 40–41
  selection problem in, 41
Permanent addressing framework. *See* Fixed addressing
Perpendicular, 16
Pitts, W., 8, 35
Planning, 106, 108
Pointer chain, 79, 101
Pole, 17, 19
Prediction, 80–86, 98
  higher order, 83–86
  multifold, 84–85
  multiorder, 89
  multistep, 86
Preference, preference function, 107–108, 111
  built-in, 109

154   Index

Preference, preference function (cont.)
  extending of, 109–111
  realizing of, 109
Purkinje cell, 10–11, 91–95
Pylyshyn, Z. W., 113

Reading
  at an address, 65, 67
  iterated, 68–70
  from memory, 30
Record of the past. See Memory record
Rehearsal, 77
Reliability, internal and external measures of, 77 83
Response region, 43–46
  shape of, 48
  size of, 47
Reward, and punishment, 111
Reward mechanism, internal, 112
Robotics, 112, 120
Role model, 110, 112
  identifying with, 112
Rosenberg, C. R., 11
Rosenblatt, F., 9, 11, 38
Rumelhart, D. E., 11

Scale model, 99, 113–114
Schank, R. C., 111
Sejnowski, T. J., 11
Selecting as computing. See Address decoding
Self, in modeling others, 112
Semantic-net models, 11
Semantic space, 2, 14, 25. See also Memory space
  distribution of, 33
Sensory component, 103–106
Sequence recognition, 98
  rhythm vs. tempo in, 86
Sequences, 26
  learning of, 79–86
  storage and retrieval of, 3
Sequential access, 2, 4, 13
Serial vs. parallel computing, 52
Set, 26
Signal-to-noise ratio, 71, 138
Signal strength, 71
Similar, 16
Similarity of concepts. See Semantic space
Similarity of memory items. See Semantic space

Sparseness, 51, 53–59
Sphere analogy, 17–18
Stellate cell, 91–93
Stimulus, 106
Stimulus-response theory, 81, 110
Stonham, T. J., 11
Storage location, 30, 32–33. See also Hard location
  capacity of, 66, 74–75
Structure vs. function, 6–7
Sum
  pooled, 77
  weighted, 36, 43–44
Sum pattern, 102
Suppes, Patrick, 27
Symbols, structure of, 118
Synapses, 35
  adjustable, 88
  as bit location, 88
  excitatory and inhibitory, 8, 35
Synaptic theory of signal transmission, 8
Synaptic weight, 35
Szentagothai, J., 91

Thagard, P. R., 109
Threshold, 35
  and response region, 44
Thurber, K. J., 33
Time, in memory trace, 14, 79
Tip-of-the-tongue phenomenon, 2, 76–77
Transition, 81
  first order, 81
  higher order, 83, 84
  multistep, 84
Triangle, third side of, 19, 21, 121–124
Trie memory, 12–13
Turing machine, 6, 52

Unexpected event, 111
Unifying principle, 14, 49, 79
Unit cube, 17

von Neumann, J., 9

Widrow, B., 11
Wilczek, F., 11
Williams, R. J., 11
Willshaw, D. J., 11
Word, at an address, 65
World model. See Internal model of the world

Write addresses, 98
Writing
 with an address, 64
 into a location, 64
 into memory, 30